Purposeful Leadership:
Building a Legacy and Lasting Impact

by

Dan Miller

Tad Dickel, PhD	Myhriah Young
Colleen Law, PhD	Ron Price, MA
James Woosley	John Buchy
Amy S. Hamilton, PhD	Amanda Kelly
Joanna Hioe	Lee Brower
Renee Metty	Phyllis Jenkins
Rev. Charity Goodwin	Shylla Webb
Phil Mershon	Cosette Leary
Kent Sanders	Jennifer Harshman

Harshman Services

P.O.Box 82

Spring Valley, IL 61362

harshmanservices.com

Printed in the United States of America

Contents

Introduction

Purposeful leadership centers around aligning the tasks and objectives of a team or organization with a distinct and profound purpose. Purposeful leaders have a visionary outlook that transcends immediate gains and profits, aiming to serve their employees, customers, and the broader world. Achieving effective purposeful leadership requires a profound comprehension of the organization's purpose, values, and objectives.

These leaders are beacons of inspiration and motivation. They communicate their vision with unwavering clarity and conviction, leading by example and embodying the values and behaviors they expect from their team. Purposeful leaders cultivate an environment conducive to innovation and continual growth, fostering a culture that encourages risk-taking, exploration of ideas, and learning from both triumphs and setbacks. They provide their team with the resources, support, and constructive feedback needed to attain their objectives.

Effective purposeful leaders exhibit visionary thinking, foster innovation, and offer unwavering support. They are driven by the desire to generate positive impacts on their team, customers, and society as a whole. The essence of this book lies in crafting a clear and captivating vision for an organization, aligning the team's pursuits and aspirations with that vision, and inspiring and motivating them to forge ahead together in pursuit of a shared purpose.

Within these pages, you will discover invaluable insights and advice from today's purposeful leaders. Use this resource to develop your own unique style of purposeful leadership and make a transformative impact within your organization and beyond. By investing in your team, fostering an environment that embraces innovation, and measuring success beyond mere financial metrics, you will leave an indelible legacy as a purposeful leader committed to making a meaningful difference.

A Note from Dan Miller

I firmly believe that when you align your passions, talents, and values with a sense of purpose, incredible things start to happen in your life and the lives of those around you.

To be clear, becoming a purposeful leader is not about holding a fancy title or occupying a high-level position within an organization. It's about how you show up every day, regardless of your role or circumstances. It's about leading with intention, authenticity, and a deep sense of meaning.

First and foremost, discovering your purpose is essential. It's about understanding what truly drives you, what brings you joy, and what impact you want to make in the world. Take some time to reflect on your strengths, interests, and the values that guide your decision-making. Ask yourself, "What would I do if money were not a factor? How can I use my talents to serve others?" These questions will help you uncover your purpose and set the foundation for your leadership journey.

Once you've clarified your purpose, it's time to step into the role of a leader. Remember that leadership is not about bossing people around or exerting control. It's about inspiring, empowering, and serving others. Purposeful leaders understand that their primary responsibility is to create an environment where their team members can thrive and contribute their best.

To become a purposeful leader, focus on developing your emotional intelligence. This means cultivating self-awareness, empathy, and effective communication skills. Take the time to understand your own emotions and triggers, and learn how to manage them effectively. Tune in to the needs and perspectives of those around you, and seek to understand before being understood.

People connect with authenticity and want to follow someone who is genuine and transparent. So share your successes and failures, and be open to learning from others. I often share the story of how I failed at running a gym, went deep into debt because of it, and had to work hard to recover. This vulnerability builds trust and encourages a culture of continuous growth and improvement.

Chapter 1: Power and Prerequisites of Purposeful Leadership

"Great leaders are willing to sacrifice their personal
interests for the greater good."
—Simon Sinek,
*Start with Why: How Great Leaders Inspire Everyone
to Take Action*

The power of purposeful leadership lies in its ability to align individuals, teams, and organizations around a clear and meaningful aim. Purposeful leaders inspire and motivate their teams toward a common goal, creating a sense of shared purpose and significance that goes beyond short-term gains and profits.

This approach has a significant impact on an organization's performance and success, driving innovation, improving employee engagement, and increasing customer loyalty. It creates a culture of trust and collaboration, where individuals are empowered to take ownership and initiative and where failure is seen as an opportunity for learning and growth.

It can also have a positive impact on society as a whole, as purposeful leaders often have a vision that goes beyond their organization's bottom line. They strive to make a difference in their communities and the world at large, using their influence and resources to address social and environmental issues and to create a more sustainable and equitable future. With purposeful leadership, everyone can work toward a shared vision that benefits both the organization and the world.

> Embrace the power of purposeful leadership. Your vision can transform reality.

Benefits for Individuals, Teams, and Organizations

Purposeful leadership brings forth numerous advantages for individuals, teams, and organizations, fostering a thriving environment where everyone can flourish.

For individuals

Aligning with a clear purpose instills a heightened sense of meaning and fulfillment in their work, enabling them to find deeper satisfaction and purpose in what they do. Purposeful leaders serve as a catalyst, inspiring and motivating their team members by creating a shared sense of purpose and meaning. This, in turn, amplifies employee motivation and engagement, leading to higher levels of productivity and commitment.

For teams

Purposeful leadership empowers individuals within the team, granting them a greater sense of autonomy and empowerment. By placing trust in their team members and encouraging them to take ownership of their work, purposeful leaders enable individuals to make decisions that align with the organization's purpose and values. This autonomy not only enhances job satisfaction but also fosters personal growth and development.

For organizations

Enhanced competitiveness, financial success, and a positive reputation are benefits organizations experience. This kind of leadership attracts and retains talented individuals by nurturing a culture of fulfillment. Ultimately, purposeful leadership unlocks the full potential of teams and organizations, creating a ripple effect of collaboration, innovation, and positive impact on both individuals and the world.

Other Styles

Purposeful leadership differs from other leadership styles in several key ways. Here are some of the main differences.

Focus on purpose: Purposeful leadership is centered around a clear and meaningful purpose that guides decision-making and actions. Other leadership styles may focus on different priorities, such as profit, power, or personal success.

Empowerment and collaboration: Purposeful leaders trust and empower their team members to take ownership and initiative, and they foster a culture of collaboration and communication. Other leadership styles may be more directive or authoritarian, with less emphasis on collaboration and empowerment.

Long-term focus: Purposeful leadership takes a long-term view, prioritizing sustainable growth and positive impact over short-term gains or quick fixes. Other leadership styles may prioritize short-term results or personal gain.

Emphasis on values: Purposeful leadership is guided by a set of core values that inform decision-making and behavior. Other leadership styles may not place as much emphasis on values or may prioritize different values.

Inclusive and diverse: Purposeful leaders value diversity and inclusivity, recognizing the importance of different perspectives and experiences. Other leadership styles may be more exclusive or homogeneous.

Purposeful leaders align their actions and goals with a clear and meaningful purpose, inspiring and motivating others, and making a positive difference in the world.

First Things First by Amanda Kelly

"Don't let your essential be at the mercy of the
very important."
—Lee Brower

In the dynamic world of business, entrepreneurs and other leaders often find themselves overwhelmed by a multitude of competing directives, hindering their ability to complete projects and achieve desired outcomes. The absence of a deliberate plan of execution further exacerbates this challenge. To overcome these obstacles and thrive as purposeful leaders, it is crucial to gain a deep understanding of our true vision and essential commitments. By aligning our actions with purpose, we embody the qualities of effective leadership and inspire our teams to wholeheartedly support our mission.

As leaders, it is our responsibility to understand what we are genuinely striving to accomplish and the purpose that drives our endeavors. By clearly articulating our essential commitments, we empower our teams to stand alongside us and help fulfill these objectives.

Indecision is a silent disruptor that can erode the foundation of effective leadership. Leaders who struggle to make necessary decisions, postpone them until the last minute, or exhibit inconsistent decision-making create a ripple effect of negative consequences. Team members lose confidence in their leader's abilities, feeling ill-equipped to make meaningful progress. The behavior erodes morale over time, diminishing the team's overall effectiveness. By surrounding ourselves with the right people and fostering an environment of gratitude and strong work ethic, we lay the groundwork for success. Providing clear direction equips every team member to perform at their best.

Entrepreneurs known for their ability to generate groundbreaking ideas often face the challenge of executing these concepts successfully. With numerous tasks competing for their attention, bringing these ideas to fruition becomes increasingly difficult. As leaders, it is essential to allocate time to evaluate each idea critically. By determining whether an idea aligns with our highest purpose and honors our essential commitments, we ensure that our efforts are focused on what truly matters. Lee Brower's insightful distinction between the very important and the essential reminds us that a true vision allows us to say no to even the most seemingly urgent matters, prioritizing what truly drives us.

Saying yes to one endeavor inherently means saying no to something else. Acknowledging this reality is crucial for effective leadership. Realistically, there are limits to what we can accomplish within a given timeframe. By establishing reasonable parameters and prioritizing our commitments, we can maintain focus and achieve our most significant goals. This does not imply shying away from ambitious aspirations or grand plans. Rather, it necessitates identifying key objectives that, once accomplished, will create a domino effect, facilitating success in other areas. Adopting a mindset of going deep, not wide, allows us to channel our energy toward endeavors that yield the highest rewards.

When faced with decisions, it is essential to evaluate their impact on our business, team, and personal life. We must ask ourselves what the biggest difference is that each decision will make and envision the best possible outcome. Clearly outlining decisions and setting a desired timeline for completion is paramount. Recognizing that we cannot do everything at once, we establish reasonable parameters and prioritize our commitments. By staying organized and keeping track of essential tasks, we ensure successful completion even with competing demands. Remember, while we can't do everything, we can focus on what we can do and execute it effectively.

Every action you take as a purposeful leader has the potential to create a wave of positve change that extends far beyond your immediate reach.
Be intentional.

In the pursuit of success, it's valuable to assess and refine our existing systems. Rather than discarding everything when something doesn't go according to plan, we should identify the components that worked, and retain them. By carefully evaluating our processes, we can build upon our strengths, save time, and gain a deeper understanding of our business. It is crucial to remember that the intentionality behind the execution of using tools matters far more than the specific tools themselves. With a purposeful approach, we can make the most of our resources and maximize efficiency.

In addition to effective decision-making, adequate preparation is vital for a successful journey. Planning is essential for a smooth trip and equally important in the realm of business decisions. Without proper preparation, we are forced to make hasty decisions along the way, leading to increased challenges and costs. By dedicating time at the beginning of our journey to prepare, we avoid unnecessary setbacks and ensure a more seamless path to success. This metaphorical approach to business decisions emphasizes the significance of foresight and deliberate planning.

Each new day presents us with the opportunity to improve and make a positive impact. In the pursuit of progress, prioritize growth over perfection. A prime example of this mindset can be found in Apple's approach to launching the iPhone 1.0. Recognizing that it wasn't the pinnacle of perfection, they made a deliberate decision to release it and subsequently focused on continuous improvement, leading to the development of iPhone 2.0 and beyond. This mentality of embracing iterative advancements can be applied to your own endeavors.

When embarking on a new journey, following a set path can greatly enhance your chances of success. By considering the following A New Dae steps, you can navigate the path of progress with purpose:

Decide. Begin by clearly defining your objective, establishing a realistic timeline, and envisioning the best possible outcome. It is crucial to assess whether this aligns with your essential commitments. Alignment ensures that your efforts are in harmony with your overarching purpose, allowing you to stay focused on what truly matters.

Assess. Next, conduct a comprehensive assessment of the resources and requirements necessary to achieve your objective. Determine the success criteria that will guide your progress. By setting clear benchmarks, you can monitor your advancement and make adjustments as needed.

Evaluate. Take stock of what you already have in place that supports your success. Identify the aspects of your existing infrastructure, processes, and strategies that contribute positively to your goals. Simultaneously, evaluate what may be missing or could be enhanced to facilitate greater success. This allows you to build upon your strengths and fill any gaps that may hinder progress.

Delegate. Recognize the value of collaboration and identify areas that can be delegated to trusted partners. Assess who within your network possesses the skills and expertise to support you effectively. Delegating tasks and responsibilities allows you to leverage collective strengths, freeing up valuable time and energy for more strategic endeavors.

Automate. Explore the potential for automation within your operations. Consider the technology platforms available and how they can optimize your workflow. By embracing automation, you can streamline processes, increase efficiency, and free up resources for more high-value activities.

Eliminate. Determine what elements are unnecessary for success and have the courage to eliminate them. Often, we hold onto practices or processes that no longer serve our objectives. By letting go of what is no longer essential, you create space for innovation, growth, and more effective allocation of resources.

Then, implement Your Plan 1.0: Put your plan into action, executing the initial version with intentionality. Remember that this is just the starting point and the foundation for further iterations. By taking the first step and implementing your plan, you lay the groundwork for future progress.

Document. As you execute your plan, document each step and decision-making process. By capturing your actions in writing, you create a valuable reference point for future reflection, analysis, and improvement. Documentation serves as a roadmap of your journey, aiding in the continuous refinement of your approach.

Execute. Move your plan from theory to action, following the written documentation closely. By aligning your execution with your documented plan, you maintain clarity, consistency, and accountability. This adherence to your vision ensures that your actions remain in harmony with your essential commitments.

Do a Wisdom Check™. Periodically pause to assess whether your current actions still align with your purpose and goals. The Wisdom Check™ allows you to reflect on your progress, evaluate any necessary adjustments, and course correct if needed. This step ensures that you stay on the path of purposeful advancement.

Set Milestones. Setting milestones along your journey help you track progress and maintain motivation. As you reach each milestone, take a moment to acknowledge your accomplishments and reflect on the distance you have covered. These milestones serve as signposts, guiding your path and providing a sense of achievement.

Reaching a milestone should not mark the end of your journey. Instead, view each milestone as a stepping stone toward even greater heights. Once you achieve a milestone, set your sights on new horizons and establish fresh objectives. This continuous pursuit of improvement and growth ensures that you remain engaged and constantly strive for excellence. By consistently setting new milestones, you create a roadmap for ongoing progress and development.

Finish in Gratitude. Celebration and gratitude are pivotal aspects of purposeful leadership. As you approach the culmination of a significant project or reach a major milestone, take the time to celebrate your achievements and express gratitude to everyone who contributed to your success. Recognize and appreciate the efforts of your team, partners, and supporters who have been instrumental in your journey.

Celebration not only provides a well-deserved reward for your hard work but also serves as a reminder of the progress you have made. It reinforces a positive and optimistic mindset, fostering a culture of achievement within your organization. By celebrating milestones, you create a sense of accomplishment and fulfillment among team members, promoting a shared sense of purpose and camaraderie.

Moreover, progress is not solely measured by looking ahead but also by reflecting on how far you have come. Take the time to review your journey, acknowledging the obstacles you overcame, the lessons learned, and the growth you have experienced. Embrace gratitude for the experiences and individuals who have contributed to your success, cultivating a mindset of appreciation and humility.

In the ever-evolving landscape of business, effective leadership is a prerequisite for success. The ability to make deliberate decisions, align actions with purpose, and prioritize essential commitments distinguishes purposeful leaders. By understanding our vision and surrounding ourselves with the right people, we lay a strong foundation for progress. Embracing a mindset of going deep, not wide, allows us to channel our energy toward endeavors that truly matter. With careful planning, assessment, and continuous improvement, we can navigate the path of progress with purpose. Celebrating milestones and expressing gratitude for the journey reinforces a positive mindset and fosters a culture of achievement. By embracing these principles, leaders can inspire their teams, drive meaningful progress, and achieve their highest aspirations. This is the power of purposeful leadership.

Self-Leadership by Joanna Hioe

Leading Self and Others without an Official Leadership Position

Growing up, I was in the drama club at school. I was not cast in big roles, though I did have significant supporting roles and ended up learning various aspects of production. I spent much time waiting in the wings of the stage.

Gifts

The gift of being in the wings

Once, I had to close the curtain at a key point in the show. Easy, right? It was so easy—or so I thought—that I ended up chatting backstage and missing the moment. I remember how furious my teacher was. The adage of Konstantin Stanislavski, known as the father of modern acting, became real to me that day: "There are no small parts, only small actors."

Sometimes, as younger or aspiring leaders, we find ourselves "waiting in the wings" of leadership. We have a spot on the team but without a leadership title. We're the extras, the stage hands, the understudies. We're the ones who know all the lines so we won't miss a cue. Sometimes, we gaze at the people in the spotlight as we wait in the dark wondering when it will be our turn to be promoted and shine.

But what if "waiting in the wings" is the position you were meant to be in?

Now, I'm not saying that it's a permanent station and that we should not aspire to grow beyond, seek career progression, and try our hand at other roles. I'm in agreement with advice that stresses the importance of taking on "stepping stones" or temporary jobs to gain experience, insight, and practice on the way to a dream role.

What I'm suggesting is this: what if we treated this season as the gift that it is? It's the opportunity to be hidden and serve, to grow ourselves outside the pressure of the spotlight. It's a chance to practice self-leadership.

Who we choose to be in these moments might be more important than we think. If you believe that you don't have anyone following you, think again. There's always at least one person: you.

The good and bad news is that we never stop leading ourselves. The hardest person to lead is often ourselves. The question is: given a choice, would you follow you?

We can never lead beyond who we are. When we are thrust into the spotlight of leadership, our strengths and weaknesses are amplified in full view. Failure to rehearse enough could lead to forgetting a line at a crucial moment on stage. Lack of private discipline and character can lead to disastrous results in the hour we are called upon.

How much are we willing to allow ourselves to be formed while we are waiting in the wings? That can determine our performance later.

The gift of being positioned to see

"Lights."

One of the roles I had in drama was doing the lights and sound. "Lights" would be the cue in the script for me to turn up the brightness from the booth behind the audience. I grew to love lights and sound, the invisible hands that tie a story together. I could set the atmosphere with music and shine the spotlight on the main characters. Equally, I learned the power of silence and how to watch for stray stage hands in the middle of a transition.

It taught me to see others.

It helped me to be comfortable with seeing others without being seen.

It positioned me to gain perspective.

A couple of years after waiting in the wings doing backstage work, having minor acting roles, and spending time in the lighting booth, I directed. The perspective I had gained from being in those other roles allowed me to see the bigger picture and bring all aspects of a production together. Through coaching actors, I could be part of bringing a character to life. By encouraging others, I could be part of building a team that could reach its potential.

The times of hiddenness had allowed me to see things from the outside. It cultivated my heart to communicate with people across departments. It helped me develop humility as I depended on others and a hunger to grow so I could give my best. Leadership guru John Maxwell uses a musical metaphor to describe this, calling it a shift in focus "from soloist to conductor" through adding value to others, and focusing on giving instead of receiving. As he says, "One is too small a number to achieve greatness." Focusing on the big picture often leads to compounding results.

The gift of being hidden positions us to see. Here are three practical ways to maximize this season:

Keep showing up. Sometimes, we are presented with opportunities simply because we are in the room. Showing up allows us to experience team culture. It gives us an opportunity to listen to and learn from those on our team. Most of all, showing up well builds personal discipline as we embrace the rules of the game we are in.

Find a need and fill it. There is a need you can meet, somewhere. Sometimes, we want to do something impactful and visible that shows off our gifts. But character is demonstrated and trust earned in the small battles of life. Are you willing to help a colleague take a call? Buy food when team members are busy? Pick up litter? Start serving wherever you are, and you can create an environment for yourself and others to thrive. Do it even if no one knows it's you who did it.

Choose to be a multiplier. When you've learned something, practice it. When you have a unique skillset, teach it to someone. When you've walked through a phase, help someone new. Invest your talents in making the team better, and give without keeping score. While our natural tendency is to hoard what we have, generosity can lead to compounding returns and has the potential to attract mentors who want to invest in you. Who doesn't want to invest in someone who makes the people around them better?

As we grow as leaders even without a title, we gain perspective in this season that allows us to serve into subsequent ones.

The gift of being positioned to help

Service is a key that unlocks destiny. We are all the protagonists in our own lives. Despite this, we often find ourselves as a supporting character serving a bigger story.

Some roles, I was cast in more naturally. Some roles, I was not chosen for. Having been on both sides of the auditioning panel, I know the choice is often not personal; it's simply a question of who can play the role best. I usually played not the main character but a supporting character who had a big impact.

A supporting character is not a second-class role. It may be less visible, but that does not make it any less valuable. When you are serving your boss, team leader, or pastor in a support role, it is in fact an assignment that requires full investment and use of talent, energy, and skill. We need to keep doing the next right thing, so that we remain in alignment with the mission of our team and the leader we are serving under.

Speaking to graduates of Howard University, preacher, filmmaker, and entrepreneur T.D. Jakes said, "Your gift will get you in the room, but you need to own the room you're in." In other words, your abilities will get you through the audition. However, we need to take ownership if we want our impact to last. "Owning the room" does not need to be a self-centered act. In fact, "owning the room" as a supporting character can create powerful precedents for those around us, most of whom are supporting characters, too. In the *Craig Goreschel Leadership Podcast*, multi-site church pastor Craig Goreschel calls this form of support "leading up." You can "lead up" with personal power even if you do not have positional power. As we do so, we can propel our leader's vision forward.

Supporting Character

Not everyone gets a lead role every time. Here are some ways to be a good supporting character.

1. Encourage your leader; don't murmur about them. It is easy to criticize. It is far more difficult to be, as Theodore Roosevelt calls it, "the man in the arena." We do not fully understand what our leaders are going through until we sit in their seat and see things through their eyes. We reap what we sow. Let's be the followers we hope to have when it is our turn to lead: teachable people who show honor even as we communicate upward with initiative, care, and concern.

2. Get to know his or her strengths and weaknesses, and complement them with your gifts. In the words of space-bound entrepreneur and innovator Elon Musk, "You are paid in direct proportion to the difficulty of the problems that you solve." While we show up and add value in small ways, let's also use our season of relative invisibility to spot problems and solve them. Catching small problems early could be key to avoiding or managing them later on.

3. Understand their communication style to minimize friction. This is critical in communicating solutions in a form that is palatable and useful. Speaking too hastily could come across as ego. Approach the subject with humility, after discussing with appropriate advisors, and pick the right time and place to communicate your ideas, with the right attitude: to serve.

The gift of being positioned to stretch

Acting requires getting into character. This means putting yourself in the shoes of a 40-year-old professor, or a 33-year-old grocery store owner, or an 80-year-old grandma and imagining the full trajectory of their lives, even if you have not been there before.

One piece of advice I came across is to read more in order to gain access into the life experiences of others. Having a broad vocabulary of experiences allows us to express that when we are called upon. It positions us to stretch further so that we can give more of ourselves.

As John Maxwell often says, "You can't give what you don't have." The more you have, the more you can give.

Each time I'm put in a position of greater responsibility, I either find myself thankful for the preparation I was willing to put myself through or wishing that I had done more so that I would be able to contribute well.

In times of trouble, you are down to your reflexes, and in emergency situations, who you are shows. It's who you are when no one is watching that counts.

Levels of Leadership

John Maxwell notes that there are five levels of leadership.

Level 1: Position: People follow you because they have to.

Level 2: Permission: People follow you because they want to.

Level 3: Production: People follow you because of what you have done for the organization.

Level 4: People Development: People follow you because of what you have done for them personally.

Level 5: Personhood (Pinnacle): People follow you because of who you are.

One challenge faced in moving through the five levels of leadership is earning each level of leadership with each person that he or she is leading. While it may be tempting to take a shortcut with a leadership title alone, without the deep foundation of character, it will not last. As we work on who we are on the inside— our character—we eventually become the purposeful leaders that others are willing to follow, with or without a title.

Case Study: Becoming a Purposeful Leader by Colleen Law, PhD

When I was invited to write a segment for this book, I thought long and hard about what to write. I settled on a case study of someone's journey toward becoming a purposeful leader. Purposeful leadership is a special approach that goes beyond traditional leadership and seeks to positively impact not just individuals and organizations but also teams, organizations, and society. There are key traits purposeful leaders have. Someone else will write about those. I want to enter the case study.

The case study is Evie's story about her road toward becoming a purposeful leader. I write about Evie's journey because it represents a completely different way of being than she originally imagined. While people see her as a leader, she has yet to agree that she is one. I believe a story of a budding purposeful leader might encourage some and ease the minds of others. I think most people start down the road of purposeful leadership without knowing it, but don't make the mistake of thinking it is an accident that someone becomes a purposeful leader. It is actually a lifelong process involving diligent self-reflection, ongoing professional and personal development, and intentional decision-making.

Without knowing it, Evie started this process several years ago when she enrolled in Dan Miller's 48 Days to the Work You Love seminar. She joined the seminar because, like many others, she was personally and professionally unfulfilled. The seminar helped Evie name her passions, identify her personal values, label her interests, and specify the causes that inspired her. She came away from the seminar with a new self-awareness and the knowledge that she would only find fulfillment, personally and professionally, when her work reflected her values. In 2020, Evie did something she never would have done prior to attending the seminar. She decided to investigate creating the work and life she wanted rather than staying in a career that was not allowing her to express and live her values. To create this life and work, she joined the 48 Days Eagles Community, where she solidified her passions, values, and interests.

This large collection of like-minded people helped Evie learn more about herself, her strengths, her skills, and, perhaps most importantly, the sacrifices she was willing to make to improve herself and her life. The community became a large part of her network, assisted in her change from a scarcity mindset to an abundance mindset, and helped her develop the idea that would become her first business.

Evie developed a clear, compelling vision for a business designed to help dissertation students who, just as she had, experienced a gap in their graduate (PhD) education and only had one year to complete the dissertation when they returned. This business allows her to constantly learn new things, assist people to reach what is often the pinnacle of their education, spread knowledge about various topics to those who normally would not get a chance to learn about the topics, help people build a life they love that is consistent with their values, and add to society's social capital.

Interacting with purposeful leaders helped Evie develop key skills and gave her opportunities to practice those skills. She took advantage of those opportunities that gave her increased confidence—confidence that continues to help her today as a dissertation coach. As you may already know or may learn from reading this book, taking advantage of learning opportunities is a hallmark of a purposeful leader.

Evie, accepting that she has information and ideas that others need, felt she had to learn more about building, developing, and scaling her business. Here were her key questions:

- How do you make sure that your business does what it was intended to do when you developed it?

- How do you structure a business such that important values are intrinsic to the business?
- How do you expand your business to address the needs and challenges society members face?

These were hard questions to answer. Luckily, a good friend introduced her to another group of like-minded people, Platform Launchers, headed by John Stange. With the help of that group of purposeful leaders, Evie made more progress:

- She made iterative changes in both the structure and function of her business.
- She formulated plans to adapt to the changes the pandemic wrought on the work environment
- She tested new and creative ways of helping PhD candidates complete their dissertations.
- She refined her purpose and vision to ensure that her business aligned not only with her values but also with real-world needs.

At the time of this writing, Evie commented she was still on her journey toward becoming a purposeful leader. She has developed a mission and purpose for her business that is set to positively impact the lives of all clients her business serves.

Evie's business, ABD Coaching Solution, is based on establishing genuine connection with its clients. Transparency, resilience, empathy, and empowerment are the fruit of the "tree" she planted as the vision of ABD Coaching Solutions. Not only do her clients receive these fruits, so do her contracted coaches.

Evie is certain had she not enrolled in the seminar, she would not have become the person, business owner, or budding purposeful leader that she is. That one simple decision—to take a course that might help her improve her personal and professional lives—was the start of a life change that ripples through the livers of all the people Evie connects with. By making the next right decision, Evie continues to grow, her business is starting to flourish, and she is positively impacting those in her sphere of influence.

Evie advises all who come to her to do these things:

1. Focus first on establishing deep connections with people—whether they are clients or not.
2. Be transparent. There will always be people who dislike you, who are put off by you, and who simply avoid you.

They are not the people you are trying to reach. Absolute truth is key.

3. Even when faced with challenges, focus on making the next righty decision. Even if you find it isn't right, you will be taking action and moving forward away from those challenges.

By the way, Evie is me . . . Colleen Evette Law.

Chapter Recap

Purposeful leadership is powerful because it aligns individuals, teams, and organizations around a clear and significant purpose, creating a sense of shared meaning and motivation that goes beyond short-term gains and profits. Purposeful leaders can drive innovation, improve employee engagement, and increase customer loyalty, creating a culture of trust, collaboration, and opportunities for learning and growth. Purposeful leadership can also have a positive impact on society by addressing social and environmental issues and creating a more sustainable and equitable future.

Exercises

Personal Purpose Exploration:

Reflect on your values, passions, and strengths.

Write a personal purpose statement that aligns your values and desired impact.

Connect your purpose and the positive influence you can have on others.

Organizational Purpose Mapping:

Map out your team or organization's purpose, mission, and values. Identify specific decisions that align with them and some that don't.

Call to Action

If you have not already done so, decide now to be a purposeful leader. If you're not ready to do that, finish reading the book this week, and consider it then.

Chapter 2: Emotional Intelligence

"Emotional intelligence is the ability to recognize,
understand, and manage our own emotions
and to recognize, understand, and influence the
emotions of others."
—Daniel Goleman,
Emotional Intelligence: Why It Can Matter More Than IQ

Emotional intelligence plays a critical role in purposeful leadership by helping leaders to connect with their team members on a deeper level and build strong, meaningful relationships based on mutual trust and understanding.

Leaders with emotional intelligence understand the perspectives of their team members and other stakeholders. This allows them to create a work environment that is supportive, inclusive, and empowering.

Emotional intelligence also enables leaders to regulate their own emotions and respond to situations with empathy and compassion. This means being able to stay calm under pressure, handle difficult conversations with sensitivity, and make decisions with the well-being of their team members in mind.

By practicing empathy and emotional intelligence, leaders can build stronger, more collaborative teams and create a work environment that is focused on achieving a shared purpose. Effective purposeful leadership requires emotional intelligence.

Leading with EQ by Amy Hamilton

Leading with Empathy and Emotional Intelligence

As we learned from Simon Sinek, the power of "why" motivates people. The purposeful leader needs to cultivate emotional intelligence to effectively lead through positive emotions versus tasking team members in a transactional style.

You may be asking yourself why this is important. If you are the "leader," then members should automatically follow you. This may occur in some hierarchical work situations, but they will only be doing the minimum for a transactional award. In today's modern economy, when employees find themselves in a situation with a boss who is not emotionally intelligent, they look for another position. The number-one reason people leave a position is their direct supervisor.

Purposeful leaders need emotional intelligence to be a leader that people want to follow. To be emotionally intelligent takes time and practice. Many people undervalue soft skills, and leaders are often promoted on technical merit that does not serve them well as leaders. Purposeful leaders need to be able to communicate effectively, resolve conflicts, and empower and support their team members.

Emotional intelligence helps leaders communicate effectively and display empathy. They can tune in to the emotions and needs of others, adapt their communication style accordingly, and convey their message in a way that resonates with different individuals. This skill is crucial for inspiring and motivating others toward a shared purpose.

Daniel Goleman is a psychologist and author who popularized the concept of emotional intelligence through his book *Emotional Intelligence: Why It Can Matter More Than IQ* that was published in 1995. Goleman's original model of emotional intelligence consisted of five key realms:

- **Self-awareness:** This refers to the ability to recognize and understand one's own emotions, strengths, weaknesses, and values. Self-aware leaders have a deep understanding of their own emotions, how they affect their behavior, and their impact on others.
- **Self-regulation:** This component involves managing and controlling one's emotions, impulses, and behaviors. Leaders with strong self-regulation skills can stay composed and calm in challenging situations, effectively manage stress, and respond to situations with thoughtfulness and resilience.
- **Motivation:** Motivation in the context of emotional intelligence refers to the ability to channel emotions towards achieving personal and organizational goals. Purposeful leaders with high motivation are driven, passionate, and committed. They inspire and energize their teams to perform at their best and persevere in the face of obstacles.
- **Empathy:** Empathy is the capacity to understand and share the emotions of others. Empathetic leaders are attentive listeners who genuinely understand the needs, concerns, and perspectives of their team members. They create a supportive and inclusive environment by demonstrating empathy and treating others with respect and kindness.
- **Social skills:** Social skills encompass a range of interpersonal abilities such as communication, collaboration, influence, and conflict resolution. Leaders with strong social skills excel in building and maintaining relationships, effectively communicate their ideas, inspire others, and foster a collaborative and cohesive team culture.

This traditional model of Goleman was refined to four dimensions. One key aspect of it that is difficult to learn is empathy. Empathy is the ability to understand and share the feelings, perspectives, and experiences of others. It involves the capacity to put oneself in someone else's shoes, to imagine what they might be feeling or thinking, and to respond with compassion and understanding. Empathy allows individuals to connect emotionally with others, to recognize and validate their emotions, and to respond in a supportive and caring manner.

Purposeful leaders need to be able to connect with their team members and grasp their emotional needs. Human resources are human beings who want to be valued and understood. As we go through each of the four dimensions of emotional intelligence, you may find it valuable to take breaks between each dimension. This is designed to be actionable so that you as a purposeful leader will have the skills you need to be successful.

Self-Awareness

We will begin with self-awareness. This involves recognizing and understanding one's own emotions, strengths, weaknesses, and values. It is the foundation of emotional intelligence as it allows individuals to accurately perceive and interpret their own emotional states. Self-awareness also includes an understanding of how emotions can influence thoughts and behaviors.

Mastering your self-awareness is essential to mastering the three other dimensions of emotional intelligence. Self-awareness allows you as a purposeful leader to understand your emotions in a situation and should prepare you to better handle triggering situations.

When you develop your self-awareness, you will be able to identify your emotions as they are occurring in real time. Identifying your emotions as they occur can be a critical communication skill.

Your emotions as a leader can have an impact not only on how you manage situations but how others around you handle situations as well.

Have you ever had a boss that you had to avoid because they were "in a mood?" How did you feel? Do you want to be that boss, or do you want to be a purposeful leader who inspires others?

Self-Management

Self-management refers to the ability to effectively regulate and direct one's own thoughts, emotions, behaviors, and actions to achieve desired outcomes. Self-management encompasses several key skills and behaviors, including self-awareness, self-control, time management, goal setting, motivation, stress management, and adaptability. It involves taking personal responsibility for one's choices and actions, setting goals, organizing tasks, making decisions, and monitoring progress towards those goals.

Self-management is particularly important in various aspects of life, including education, work, relationships, and personal growth. As a purposeful leader, self-management will enable you to prioritize tasks, manage time more efficiently, and demonstrate a strong work ethic to your team members. In relationships, self-management involves effective communication, empathy, and conflict resolution skills. For personal growth, self-management entails setting and pursuing meaningful goals, overcoming obstacles, and maintaining a healthy work-life balance.

By developing and practicing these skills, individuals can enhance their personal effectiveness, productivity, and overall well-being. Self-management plays a crucial role in promoting individual autonomy, resilience, and success across different domains of life. Self-regulation is built on your self-awareness.

Social Awareness

Social awareness is crucial for building and maintaining healthy relationships, effective communication, and successful collaboration. It enables purposeful leaders to understand and respect the perspectives of others, respond appropriately to social cues, and contribute positively to social environments. This is particularly important in diverse and multicultural settings.

Social awareness also involves recognizing and understanding social norms, expectations, and power dynamics. It includes understanding appropriate behavior in different social contexts and understanding how social hierarchies and structures influence interactions. Social awareness helps navigate social situations with tact and adaptability.

Your team members will be looking to you to set the social norms for your team. Your reactions and tolerances will become the unwritten standards of the group. This is why it is critical to master self-awareness and self-management.

When you are in front of your team, you need to be in control of your own emotions and react appropriately to situations.

Relationship Management

Relationship management refers to the ability to build and maintain positive and productive relationships with others. It involves effectively communicating, collaborating, resolving conflicts, and fostering mutual understanding and trust. Relationship management skills are important in various contexts, including personal relationships, professional settings, and community interactions.

As a purposeful leader, it is important to realize that team members may see you outside of the work environment and if they perceive that you are different outside of work this can erode the relationship. Relationships are built between leaders and their team members based on effective communication which leads to trust.

Effective communication is fundamental to relationship management. It involves both verbal and nonverbal communication, active listening, expressing thoughts and feelings clearly, and being attentive to the communication styles and needs of others. Good communication helps in conveying messages accurately, resolving conflicts, and building strong connections. When communications fail trust is lost.

Trust is the foundation of any healthy relationship. Relationship management involves building and maintaining trust by being reliable, honest, and acting with integrity. It requires fulfilling commitments, maintaining confidentiality, and demonstrating trustworthiness in interactions. Trust-building is crucial for establishing strong connections and fostering long-term relationships.

Relationship management includes the ability to work collaboratively with others towards shared goals. It involves being able to contribute to a team, respect diverse perspectives, and promote cooperation and synergy. Collaboration skills help in problem-solving, decision-making, and achieving common objectives. In the modern workplace team members seek out leaders that demonstrate that they are valued.

Have you ever had a boss that made all the decisions and had little respect for your input? How did you feel? Do you want to be that boss, or do you want to be a purposeful leader with great relationships that others want to emulate?

"Do the best you can until you know better. Then, when
you know better, do better."
—Maya Angelou

Case Study: Heart Matters by Reverend Charity Goodwin

Heart Matters are Hard Matters in Integral Leadership

"Soft skills" may be soft, but they're not simple. In fact, they are hard skills to master and require unlearning and relearning. Instead of devaluing skills such as self-awareness, empathy, and emotional regulation, purposeful leadership includes them in an intentional way. Holding together both hard and soft skills is key—especially when they are in tension with one another, which is often.

The easy choice is to seek the path of least resistance and miss opportunities for depth, trust, and growth. Purposeful leadership is integral. It allows one to bring and acknowledge all of who they are. In addition, purposeful leadership invites others to likewise function in holistic, integrated ways. I learned about all of this the hard way though, through the leadership school of hard knocks and mistakes.

Personality and leadership assessments shaped my early leadership experience. I had all of the letters in my email signature signaling my identity such as my DiSC profile of DI (the plotted graph characterized me as a pioneer), Myers-Briggs INTJ, and my top 5 StrengthFinders: achiever, focus, strategic, relator, and futuristic. These days, I'd add Enneagram 3 wing 4 to the alphabet soup.

Early on, my leadership lacked nuance. It was straightforward and simple: achieve the goals. Unfortunately, I used people to achieve the goals rather than invite them to join me and create buy-in. However, I had a way of relating and influencing that resulted in people saying yes to me. More often than not, it was because of *me*, not the mission they agreed to lead or serve. I later learned that centralizing myself in this way over the real mission was neither healthy nor sustainable.

For example, the pioneer revealed in my DiSC profile alludes to my being able to get things done with people regardless of their being a map or method. If I had to create the way, I would gladly do so. Serving as a pastor in established churches with deep tradition and institutionalization, my fresh spirit was often welcomed, but only to the extent that neither things nor people would need to change. In addition, I was quick to get down to business while missing opportunities to build trust that would last beyond a project. That would have strengthened my teams. Instead, I burned out some of them. I also did that to myself.

The Heart Attack

It was a Friday morning, and I had returned home from dropping my sons at daycare. My plan was to peruse a couple of estate sales after keeping my regular therapy appointment. While brushing my teeth, I felt a sharp pain shoot up my back. The pain receded, and I moved on until it came back stronger.

It was 9 a.m. and I began to worry that *if* it were serious—a heart attack or stroke—no one would find me until 5 p.m. So, for the first time in my life, I dialed 911.

The EMTs arrived and checked my vitals and plugged me up to a mini EKG machine. The graphs reported that I had not had a heart attack. I breathed a little easier as the pain had subsided and the report was good news. I started thinking, *Estate sales, here I come*.

Just then an EMT asked, "Ma'am, is it possible you're under some stress?" In my mind I was thinking (I'm a pastor, but some ungodly words crossed my mind): *Stress? Um, yeah, I'm stressed*. I was an associate pastor at two churches. I had two small kids; one had been recently diagnosed with autism. My then-husband and I were trying to figure out parenting and marriage. I was absolutely stressed!

That day, I learned heart attacks aren't just physical. They are also emotional. I reflect on that day as the time I had an emotional heart attack. Have you ever had a "heart attack"?

Heart matters are hard matters.

The way I had been handling my heart and my emotions was to avoid them or push them away. That Friday, they rose up in my body in pain and panic. Dr. Brené Brown, Huffington Foundation Endowed Chair at the Graduate College of Social Work, says it this way: "The body gets first crack at our emotions." We *feel* something before we think or act on it.

All of that was the beginning of my journey to intentionally integrate soft skills into my leadership. My identity has been intricately linked with doing and performing. That's why becoming more of a BE-er than a DO-er has been a long road. A woman at church would pop into my office and say, "Pastor, you're a human being not a human doing." Much of the busyness, busy work, overcompensating, and workaholic tendencies changed after my emotional heart attack. I'm sure it was a panic attack, and I have had a handful of bad ones since 2013. As I embrace my humanity, I see more of other people's humanity in everything I do—parenting, preaching, and leading.

In the same way that I invested heavily in personality assessments, I began to learn and practice emotional intelligence. My learning has been primarily through Brené Brown's research, where I am a certified The Daring Way™ Facilitator and as a Certified EQ Practitioner and Assessor with Six Seconds (www. sixseconds.org). Now people and soft skills are the heart of my leadership. I'm more effective now than I have ever been.

One of my major stumbling blocks in fully embracing EQ was my view of feelings. Societal and church messages taught me to be leery of feelings, calling them untrustworthy and even antithetical to faith. Today, however, I believe that God made us feeling beings, and therefore feelings must be acknowledged. Moreover, Jesus cared about feelings and experienced them himself.

What Emotional Intelligence Is

According to Six Seconds, emotional intelligence, also referred to as EQ, is simply being smarter with feelings so you can develop optimal relationships with yourself and others. Furthermore, EQ is a learnable, measurable skill that improves effectiveness, relationships, quality of life, and well-being. People are assessed in all of these and more.

Let's start with what feelings are, and then I'll reveal the results of my first emotional intelligence assessment. Here are a few characteristics of feelings:

Normal: Everyone has them, and they are biologically part of humanity's DNA.

Informative: When we pay attention to them, they can give us meaningful information about what's going on inside of us. As an example, you're in a board meeting and someone says they disagree and you start to feel uncomfortable and tight, that's information to unpack. What am I feeling? What's this response? You might feel afraid to be challenged or disrespected. A myriad of other responses and feelings can arise. The key is to pay attention.

Signs: They are meant to be paid attention to not dismissed.

Neutral: Feelings are not good or bad.

Simultaneous: You can feel multiple feelings at one time (there is no need to choose).

Not the opposite of faith: I believe feelings are part of what it means to love God with our whole heart (Luke 10:27), and if we dismiss them, then we've only experienced a portion of who God is, who we are, and what is possible.

An assessment looks at competencies to glean clues about one's leadership. The Six Seconds Emotional Intelligence Assessment measures the following eight competencies:

- Enhance Emotional Literacy
- Recognize Patterns
- Apply Consequential Thinking
- Navigate Emotions
- Engage Intrinsic Motivation
- Exercise Optimism
- Increase Empathy
- Purse Noble Goal

My first EQ assessment in 2016 revealed three areas of growth: enhancing emotional literacy, navigating emotions, and increasing empathy.

Before emotional intelligence, not only did I not acknowledge feelings, but I also didn't have an emotional vocabulary. I was comfortable expressing three feelings: happiness, sadness, and anger. Using various feeling wheels, I learned that there is a plethora of feelings I had experienced but didn't have the words to describe.

Enhancing Emotional Literacy

Have you ever said any of these?

I was in my feelings.

Sorry I got emotional.

I won't let my feelings get the best of me.

I'm just gonna have faith and not let my feelings get in the way.

Variations of these kinds of phrases diminish and discount the value of feelings. Instead of allowing feelings to inform us, we often negate them. When you practice emotional intelligence, you consciously include feelings in your decisions, leadership, and responses.

The truth is, emotions always impact our decision-making, yet we're not always aware of how. Too often when people are asked how they feel, the response is with what they think or what they're doing. Cultivating an emotional vocabulary allows us to access and articulate our feelings rather than our thoughts or behaviors.

What helped me was using a feelings wheel. I know, roll your eyes. I did the same thing. But that's how deficient I was; I needed prompts and aids. I still use them, and I'm not ashamed of that.

One I use is by Six Seconds. It's called Plutchik's Wheel of Emotions. It is interactive and gives even more insight with questions and videos to go further.

Here are a few ways to support emotional literacy in your leadership:

- Invite people to share one feeling word at the beginning and/or end of a meeting.
- Jot down phrases you hear along with the emotions they may be conveying. (Please note: we can't give voice to others' feelings; we can only ask, model, or suggest).
- Use a feelings wheel to check in with yourself after a meeting.

Navigating Emotions

My emotional literacy was low, and I was not navigating my feelings in part because I hardly knew what I was feeling. Those feelings were information, data that could have helped me in navigating conflict, building trust, or making decisions.

Navigating emotions is when we access, generate, or transform emotions. If you're anything like me, you might be skeptical that this is even possible. I, too, didn't buy it at first. It took me months before I had a transformed emotion. I had to focus first on embracing the feelings I experienced and giving them a name.

After trusting that feelings were not the enemy, I began to generate my emotions. Note this might sound like bypassing. It's not. One experiences a wide range of emotions. The first time I generated an emotion, I was practicing emotional intelligence. I read about how to generate an emotion, and I tried it. The emotion I was feeling was disrespected, dismissed. From there, I asked myself which feeling I wanted to feel. The answer was respected, admired, acknowledged. I spent time allowing myself to recall having felt the pride of being respected. The posture of respect was in my body, and I remembered what it means to admire and be admired.

Next, I reviewed the original disrespectful scenario, and the emotion I felt was proud. I then reflected on a response to the scenario from a completely different place of pride and acknowledgment.

This takes time to learn, let alone master. I'm not there yet. But I have tools of emotional intelligence that support me in leading in a healthy and more purposeful way.

Here are two ways to practice navigating emotions in your leadership:

- Wait six seconds before responding.
- Use Think Feel Act™ Cards from Six Seconds to address and generate emotions.

Increasing Empathy

"People don't care how much you know until they know how much you care." This quotation has been attributed to many people, including Theodore Roosevelt. I remember hearing it for the first time in leadership training and thinking, *I've got some work to do.* Unfortunately, I went to a different extreme of caring so that I could get things done through people. My care wasn't genuine.

Fast forward to today. The opportunity to show care and concern for people is one I see quite differently now. Another way to talk about this is empathy.

Empathy is appropriately acknowledging and responding to others' feelings. Empathy is key to understanding others and forming enduring and trusting relationships. It ensures you take other people into account in your decision-making and gives them a rock-solid assurance that you are on the same team, according to Six Seconds.

When I received my leadership results showing empathy as a growth area, I was embarrassed. I'm a pastor, for goodness' sake. Then I learned two things: 1) Empathy is expressed toward others as well as one's self and 2) Among my pastor clients, empathy consistently shows up as in the bottom three competencies. When we discuss the two directions of empathy, they're comforted in a way. Typically, the response is "Okay, that makes sense." It is as if to say, "at least I have empathy toward others," clearly demonstrating the lack of self-empathy in that moment. Other times, pastors are so production driven that they forget about the people side of ministry.

> **Authenticity and empathy will earn the trust of your team.**

With emotional intelligence, we bring both productivity and people together in our leadership posture. While it won't be perfect, it's worth trying because at the heart of leadership is people— people who do the work, people we serve, people such as family and friends whose support matters deeply, and also one person you take with you wherever you go: you.

The Goal of Integration

I've lived at the ends of two extremes in my leadership: doing and thinking, focused on what I achieved with my hands as well as what I thought in my head. Now, I'm convinced that there is a more excellent way.

The Bible story of Mary, Martha, and Jesus in Luke 10:38–42 has mentored me since my "heart attack" days. The story is about two sisters who receive a visit from Jesus. Martha, the older sister, who likely owns the house, is busy making preparations during Jesus's visit. Mary, on the other hand, is sitting at the Teacher's feet learning from him.

My journey had become one where I sought to no longer be a Martha and instead be like Mary. Be a be-er not a do-er. Or allow my doing to flow from my being is another way to say that.

After some years, I realized there is so much more in the passage. The story isn't just about Mary and Martha; it is also about Jesus. When Martha approaches Jesus about working while Mary sits, she asks him to make Mary help. Jesus replies, saying, "Martha, Martha. You are worried about many things." In some translations, he says "anxious." Both worried and anxious are emotions that Jesus names in this conflict ensuing before him. Jesus gets to the heart of the matter, the feelings.

For a person who's known this story much of her life, it is pure joy and challenge that Jesus would name emotions. His reply heightens the importance of emotional literacy for me. This story, much like soft skills and hard skills, has been seen as diametrically opposing. I now see the story as much more than that. It is a story about the integration of our head (Mary), heart (Jesus) and hands (Martha). Bringing all of who we are to every conversation, leadership decision, and relationship is to live integrated. This wholeness is an invitation to us. In Christian Scripture, the Greek word for salvation is *sozo*, which means whole. Therefore, for me, practicing emotional intelligence in my leadership is salvific and of extreme importance.

What's your reason for leading with heart? Why is it important to you? If it's not yet, take inventory of the benefits listed in this book. Reflect on how your leadership and life would be different by intentionally assessing and practicing emotional intelligence.

Chapter Recap

Emotional intelligence is essential for a purposeful leader. Throughout this chapter, we focused on dimensions of emotional intelligence, including self-awareness, self-management, social awareness, and relationship management. Each of these skills builds on the others. Take your time, and work on different aspects of your emotional intelligence each day.

As a purposeful leader, emotional intelligence is an essential tool in your toolkit. As you continue to read this book, consider other tools you can use. It is up to you to continue the journey. You will never be perfect, but you will be on a positive path.

Most purposeful leaders have some traits in common, mainly related to emotional intelligence. They are self-motivated, persevere through obstacles, and examine themselves, their teams, and the bigger picture to make informed decisions and learn from mistakes. Purposeful leaders manage themselves and others effectively, leading to a positive and productive environment.

Exercises

Self-Assessment:

This is the most important step in self-awareness and should be conducted periodically. If you have never done a self-awareness assessment the first time may be uncomfortable and enlightening. There are many tests you can take online or with a professional. Below are a few questions that you may use:

1. What are your three biggest strengths?
2. What are your three biggest weaknesses?
3. When was the last time you lost your temper? Why? Was it appropriate?
4. When was the last time you cried? Why? Was it appropriate?
5. When was the last time you laughed so hard it hurt? Why? Was it appropriate?
6. What is your happiest childhood memory? Saddest?

After you answer these questions, determine which areas you should work on and why.

Said, Heard, Meant:

Practice conflict resolution before it becomes an issue. Have one member make a statement directed toward another speaker. The second speaker needs to state what they heard to include how the first speaker made them feel. The first speaker responds with what they meant. Often when we are in a hurry we may come across as brisk or uncaring. Establishing intent and communication styles in your team will go a long way.

Escape Room:

Both physical and virtual escape rooms are available and a great way to create a collaborative environment for your team. These puzzle solving opportunities can allow team members who don't normally interact to interact with each other. Also challenge yourself as a leader—do the team members in your room automatically defer to you, or do they feel they can be equal partners in this environment?

Social Awareness:

Here are several ways to improve your social awareness:

- Watch a few movie clips with friends and discuss your emotional reactions. Did you perceive a situation to be tense, but your friend found that situation to be melodramatic? It is okay to perceive things differently.

- Listen to some customer service training calls. What can you learn from how other people handle stressful situations?

- Be willing to share your own emotions. Sharing your emotions, especially when they are negative or make you vulnerable, can allow others to be open with you in return. Share in a way that is respectful and appropriate for the situation.

- There are so many emojis now that it can be overwhelming. Look up different emojis and try to determine the difference between the grinning face emoji, the grinning face emoji with big eyes, and the grinning face emoji with smiling eyes. Just as there are subtle differences in emojis, there are subtle differences in people's emotions.

Call to Action

Consider which areas you need to strengthen. Then make a plan to do so. Even ten minutes a week can make a difference.

Chapter 3: Clarifying Your Purpose

"The two most important days in your life are the day you
are born and the day you find out why."
—Ernest T. Campbell, Sermon on January 25, 1970

Clarifying your purpose is a vital step in purposeful leadership, involving a profound understanding of personal values, passions, and strengths. This introspective process allows individuals to identify their true priorities and aspirations in life and career. By aligning personal purpose with a meaningful vision, individuals gain motivation, make better decisions, and experience greater fulfillment and success.

Similarly, at the organizational level, defining purpose entails identifying core values, mission, and vision, and aligning them with a clear and impactful purpose. This guides decision-making and strategy, and shapes the company's culture, all the way down to how negotiation is handled.

Author Susie Tomenchok emphasizes in her book The Art of Everyday Negotiation without Manipulation that purpose serves as the guiding light in every negotiation, and that we all negotiate multiple times a day.

A defined purpose attracts talented employees, fosters customer loyalty, and generates positive social and environmental impact. Leaders who embrace and embody their purpose are more likely to achieve success, create meaningful change, and leave a lasting legacy.

Importance of Alignment

Aligning personal and organizational purpose is a crucial aspect of modern leadership, offering several benefits. It leads to increased motivation and engagement among leaders. When personal purpose aligns with the organization's purpose, leaders experience heightened productivity, creativity, and job satisfaction, and they positively influence the organizational culture.. Purposeful leaders who align personal and organizational purpose make decisions that align with their values, goals, and vision. This lets them prioritize effectively, maintain focus on goals, and make decisions that serve the best interests of the organization and its stakeholders.

Moreover, aligning personal and organizational purpose enhances reputation and brand. Purposeful leaders are perceived as authentic, trustworthy, and committed to making a positive difference, attracting and retaining customers, partners, and employees. Additionally, purposeful leaders create positive social and environmental impact. They utilize their organization's resources, expertise, and influence to address societal and environmental challenges, leaving a lasting positive impact on the world.

Clarifying Purpose with Adventurous Exploration by Renee Metty

Welcome to an adventurous exploration of purposeful leadership, where we embark on a journey that combines the power of playfulness, creativity, and mindfulness. We will delve into the depths of clarifying your purpose as a leader, uncovering the magic that lies within you. So, put on your playful hats, embrace your inner child, and let's begin this magical adventure.

Purposeful leadership is like a magical quest where leaders set out on a mission to conquer goals that make their hearts sing. It's all about aligning the organization's vision with the leader's personal vision, creating a harmonious symphony of awesomeness. But wait, there's more! It's not just about winning for themselves; purposeful leaders bring joy and success to everyone involved. It's like throwing a party where everyone leaves with a smile.

> Be the catalyst for innovation and progress within your organization, inspiring others to think outside the box and push boundaries.

Guess what. The key to this leadership extravaganza is unlocking your purpose. It's like finding the hidden treasure map

38

that keeps you laser-focused, excited, and totally boss at achieving those amazing goals. Let the fun begin!

Embracing the Power of Playfulness

As leaders, we often get caught up in the seriousness and demands of our roles. However, playfulness holds the key to unlocking our true purpose. When we engage in play, we tap into our innate curiosity, imagination, and joy. Play allows us to break free from rigid thinking patterns, encouraging fresh perspectives and innovative solutions.

Let's take a moment to reconnect with our playful nature. Close your eyes, take a deep breath, and allow yourself to remember the pure joy of childhood games. Recall the freedom of running barefoot, the laughter of playing tag, and the exhilaration of building sandcastles. Breathe in that vibrant energy. Carry it with you as we dive deeper into clarifying your purpose.

Clarifying your purpose is the place to start. It's like getting a backstage pass to understand what gets you all fired up and gives you that extra pep in your step. It's like finding the secret sauce that keeps you motivated and pointed in the right direction. When you have a crystal-clear purpose, you become a goal-getting ninja, laser-focused and ready to conquer the world.

Clarifying your purpose isn't just about you—it's like playing matchmaker with your goals and your organization's dreams. You want everyone to be singing from the same sheet of music. Knowing your purpose helps you sync with your organization's values and vision like a perfectly choreographed dance routine.

It also turns you into a decision-making superhero. No more getting lost in the rabbit hole of distractions or juggling conflicting priorities. When you know what you want to achieve, you can make decisions that turbocharge your goals and keep you on the right track. Get ready to unleash your purposeful powers and discover a whole new level of awesomeness.

Unleashing Your Purposeful Powers

Ready to embark on a purpose-finding adventure that's more thrilling than a roller coaster ride? Buckle up, because here are some strategies to help you clarify your purpose in the magical realm of purposeful leadership.

Soul Search Shenanigans: Set aside some quality time to dig deep and explore what truly sets your soul on fire. Ask yourself those mind-boggling questions like, "What brings me joy?" or "What impact do I want to make on the world?" It's like being a detective, uncovering clues about your passions, values, and talents. Grab your magnifying glass and get ready to discover your purposeful superpowers.

Adventure with Reflection: Take a journey through the enchanted forest of self-reflection. Carve out moments to ponder and reflect on your experiences, both triumphs and challenges. What have you learned along the way? What themes and patterns emerge? It's like unraveling the plot of your own heroic story, gaining insights that lead you straight to the heart of your purpose.

Conversations of Wonder: Engage in magical conversations with mentors, friends, or even a wise old owl if you can find one. Share your thoughts, dreams, and aspirations with others. Soak up their wisdom and perspective. It's like having a brainstorming session with the dream team, gathering insights that will light up your path and reveal hidden treasures.

Passion Projects Galore: Dive headfirst into passion projects that ignite your enthusiasm and showcase your unique talents. Explore new hobbies, volunteer for causes close to your heart, or initiate projects that align with your values. It's like throwing a party where your passions are the main attraction, and your purpose is the dazzling fireworks display leaving everyone in awe.

Learning from the Masters: Delve into the stories and experiences of purposeful leaders who inspire you. Read books, listen to podcasts, attend seminars, or even go on a quest to find a wise sage who can share their insights. Let their journeys and lessons guide you, like a treasure map leading you to your own purposeful pot of gold.

Remember, clarifying your purpose is like embracing your own superhero identity. It takes time, effort, and a dash of magic. Unleash your inner explorer and embark on this grand adventure. Your purpose awaits. With these strategies in your arsenal, you'll be well on your way to greatness.

Reflecting

Let's take a lighthearted and fun approach as we reflect on your values. So often, we take this stuff too seriously. You don't have to be married to it, so consider it a work in progress, and have fun experimenting.

Cozy Corners

Imagine you're in a cozy café, sipping a delicious cup of your favorite beverage. Take a moment to ponder what truly makes you tick. What lights a fire in your soul? What gets you excited to be the rockstar leader that you are?

Grab a trusty notebook or a blank sheet of paper, and let's get down to business. But hey, no need to stress about neatness or perfection here. This is your brainstorming session. Messy scribbles are totally allowed!

Think of yourself as a detective uncovering the secret codes of your values. Jot down the things that matter most to you, those guiding principles that make you jump out of bed in the morning. It's like putting together the pieces of a puzzle that is uniquely you.

Once you have a colorful array of values on your page, let's play a game of sorting. Can you group them into categories? It's like organizing your own personal party with different themes. Maybe you'll create a "Courage Corner" for bravery, resilience, and taking bold leaps, or a "Kindness Kingdom" for empathy, compassion, and generosity.

This reflection is all about embracing your authentic self and having some fun along the way. Grab your pen, dive into this playful exploration of your values, and unlock the magic within you.

Unleashing Superpowers

Get ready to unleash your inner superhero as we embark on a quest to identify your strengths. Imagine you're in a vibrant lair, surrounded by a dazzling array of superpowers. This is your moment to shine, my friend. Grab your trusty notebook or a blank sheet of paper, and let's dive into the world of your extraordinary abilities.

Think of your strengths as your superpowers—those exceptional qualities that make you stand out as a leader. It's like taking an inventory of your own heroic arsenal. With confidence and gusto, make a glorious list of all the things you excel at. Fly high, my friend, and don't hold back.

Now, here's the twist: we're not stopping at recognition alone. We're all about making a difference, right? So, let's put on our capes and consider how we can use these magnificent strengths for good. How can you channel your powers to create an impact in your organization and community? It's like joining a league of extraordinary leaders, combining forces to make the world a better place.

Remember, this is your time to shine brightly and embrace your awesomeness. Uncover the superhero within you.

Treasure Map

Prepare to embark on a thrilling treasure hunt as you define your vision with a playful twist. Imagine you're a fearless adventurer, wielding a trusty treasure map that leads to your ultimate destination as a purposeful leader. But here's the catch: this treasure map isn't your ordinary map. It requires your vision to be clear, specific, and totally achievable. Dive into the exciting world of vision-setting with a little help from the SMART goal framework.

Think of your vision as the X that marks the spot of your grand treasure. We're not just settling for vague wishes. We're all about setting goals that are Specific, Measurable, Achievable, Relevant, and Time-Bound—the SMART way.

What does your vision look like? How will you measure your progress along the way? What steps can you take to make it happen?

Remember, your vision is your map of the path to greatness. Grab your metaphorical pirate hat, embrace your inner explorer, and define your vision using the SMART framework—because with a clear map and a playful spirit, you'll navigate the seas of purposeful leadership like a true treasure-hunting champion.

Exploring the Realm of Creativity

Creativity is the playground where purpose takes shape. It is through creative expression that we uncover our unique gifts and talents. As leaders, it is vital to tap into our creative wellsprings to fully understand our purpose and bring it to life.

Imagine your mind as a vast canvas ready to be painted with the colors of your purpose. Take a metaphorical paintbrush and let it dance across the canvas, allowing ideas, dreams, and aspirations to flow freely. Don't be afraid to mix different hues and experiment with bold strokes. Embrace the unexpected and trust the process. Remember, purpose is not a fixed destination but an evolving masterpiece.

To truly clarify your purpose, it is essential to cultivate mindfulness—a state of non-judgmental awareness and presence in the present moment. Mindfulness helps us step out of the chaos of our thoughts and connect deeply with our inner selves.

> Embrace the power of purposeful leadership.

Find a quiet space where you can sit comfortably. Close your eyes and bring your attention to your breath. Notice the sensation of each inhalation and exhalation, letting go of any tension or distractions. As you breathe, let go of expectations and simply be with what arises.

Invite your purpose to reveal itself. Allow any thoughts, feelings, or images to arise naturally. Notice the sensations in your body as you contemplate your unique contribution as a leader. Embrace the stillness and trust that the answers will come when the time is right.

Feel free to engage in creative exercises like collage-making, journaling, or even storytelling to explore these questions. Allow your imagination to run wild and embrace the unexpected connections that emerge. Remember, this is a process of self-discovery, and every layer you uncover brings you closer to the heart of your purpose.

Infusing Purpose into Leadership

Now that you have clarified your purpose, it's time to infuse it into your leadership journey. Purpose provides the compass that guides your decisions, actions, and interactions with others.

Think of purpose as the North Star that guides your leadership journey. It gives you a sense of direction and clarity, even during uncertain times.

- Embrace the power of questions.
- Seek feedback and other perspectives.
- Embrace experimentation and adaptability.
- Embody authenticity.
- Find meaning in the journey.
- Continuously revisit and refine.

Remember, clarifying your purpose as a leader is a dynamic and personal journey. It is about tapping into your inner wisdom, embracing your passions, and aligning your actions with your values. Embrace the playful, creative, and mindful aspects of this process, and let your purpose shine brightly as you lead with intention and authenticity.

This doesn't have to be dull and uninspiring. With a dash of enthusiasm and a sprinkle of imagination, you can make it energizing and invigorating. Open yourself to the possibilities, explore your values, embrace your strengths, and set goals that ignite your passion. It's like embarking on a captivating quest.

Clarifying your purpose as a leader can involve playful exploration, creative expression, and mindfulness. It is a process of self-discovery that reveals the unique contributions you bring to the world.

When you align your actions with your purpose, you can lead with intention and make a meaningful impact on those around you. Embrace your playful nature, and tap into your creativity. Cultivate mindfulness as you uncover the magic of your purpose. Happy journeying!

Clarifying Purpose with Strategic Planning by James Woosley, former PMP

Do you make plans that never get implemented? Are they so complicated they fail because you simply can't make them happen? Or do you resist planning because you just want to get things done but end up failing and reworking things more than accomplishing your goals?

Let's find the middle ground, the sweet spot that combines planning and action. What do you want to achieve? Whatever it is, it's not going to be easy. Not if it's something big worth doing right. That "something big" is a massive clue to identifying and clarifying your purpose.

The next few pages contain a summary of the Simple Strategic Planning (SSP) Framework described in detail in *Conquer the Entrepreneur's Kryptonite*. The SSP is designed to spark your ideas and set your purpose on fire—a fire under your control and direction.

Before you dig in, you should know something: The best plan in the world is worthless if it's not worth implementing. Sure, it may work, but do you want it to? Do you want to reach that destination? Or are you going through the motions, chasing someone else's dream for you, or setting out on the safe and steady path?

The most important thing you can do before making a plan of any kind is to know your purpose. Why do you want to do this? What impact will it have? Why will you smile seeing it come to fruition? Dream big. Aim high. Risk failure. Take action. Learn, and try again when it doesn't work right the first time. Persevere through the inevitable ups and downs.

Pay particular attention to Step 3 and Step 4. Your Core Values and Vision Narrative speak directly to your purpose. The rest will help you frame, communicate, and fulfill your purpose.

Note: While the info that follows is targeted toward business, it can be applied to leadership in other areas as well. Replace "business" with any other domain, and you're on your way.

A Plan for Your Business

You don't need a business plan. You need a plan for your business. First, you need to know what it is you are trying to accomplish as a leader. What are your motivations? Why do you want to do what you want to do?

It's hard to start, grow, and run a business or accomplish any meaningful goal. Living a dream doesn't happen automatically. There will be obstacles. If you're going to find a way around, over, under, or through them, you're going to need perseverance. Perseverance doesn't come from a financial reward but from passion.

Bottom line

Do a quick search on the internet for project management tools and methodologies, and you'll find hundreds if not thousands of ways to get things done. Which one is right? I can't tell you. That's because there isn't just one that works.

Many work, and some will work better for you than others do. If you're using a spreadsheet to track your finances instead of Quickbooks, you're not wrong. You have to evaluate whether what you're doing is getting the results you need or whether you can do better.

I believe the SSP can help most people do and achieve more than they have before. Will everyone like it better than what they're doing today? No. Will everyone do it the way I lay it out? No. In fact, I'm guessing most people will adjust it to fit their personal preferences. The method of doing the steps may vary, but the value of each step is clear.

SSP Overview

The Simple Strategic Planning (SSP) Framework is a systematic, straightforward process that will help you build an effective plan for your business.

It is **Simple** because it doesn't need to be complicated. Simple solutions often solve complex problems. While there are industries where project plans need to manage tens of thousands of details, that level of complexity is not needed for creating direction for a company as a whole. The SSP finds the happy middle ground between a scribble on a napkin and a detail-filled binder that's never looked at once it gets placed on a shelf.

It is **Strategic** because it forces you to think more than one step ahead but not a thousand steps ahead, considering every possible permutation. Remember that the game of checkers, while vastly easier to learn and play than chess, still has a strategy.

It is **Planning** because the result is a tangible plan you can share with your employees, coworkers, spouse, or coach. The plan outlines the step-by-step course you intend to follow to a specific outcome. It's the manifestation of your intention, and will guide you in spite of the inevitable obstacles that pop up along the way.

It is a **Framework** because it guides you through the creation of your plan for your business. No one sees the steel framework of a skyscraper once the building is completed, and the building can take whatever shape the owner desires. You are the owner. Build your plan to build your business.

Another note about skyscrapers: they sway in the wind. If they weren't flexible, they would crack and collapse. The SSP is a flexible framework because you may want to make changes to it. There are no perfect plans, so it will need to flex as you inject it into the real world.

SSP Step 1: SWOT

Building a SWOT chart is the first step in building your plan of action. Be honest in assessing each area. The rest of your strategic plan is built upon this exercise. Use simple bullet points.

- **Strengths:** Document what you do inherently well and other factors that are working in your favor. These are the good things that you can leverage to your advantage.
- **Weaknesses:** Enter the things you don't/can't do well right now. These are areas you need to develop into minimum competence or eliminate altogether as you move forward. They are present pains and are hurting your efforts.
- **Opportunities:** Write down the things that can take you to the next level once you get going. What can you tap

into to get to the next level? You will need to prioritize your activities to take advantage of these areas.

- **Threats:** List the things that are in your way or can take you down (this may include your perceived or real competitors). Counter/eliminate them while moving forward.

SSP Step 2: Mission Statement

The Mission Statement for your business taps into your passion and begins to define the dream. It should be succinct, clear, and unchanging. This is where you draw a line in the sand and give purpose to your business.

- **What does it exist for?** Use your passion. Think about the reason you wanted to start the business when it was just an idea.
- **What will it always do, even if the products and services change over time?** Think broader than the products and services you provide. Technology will change over time, and so will the needs and wants of your target market.
- **Start Writing.** Don't stare at a blank screen or sheet of paper too long. Start by writing down your thoughts, dreams, and desires for your leadership. Do mind-maps or other exercises to get going. Record yourself talking to a friend about it, and then take notes when you listen to it. Themes and keywords will start to appear.

- **Refine.** Once you get it down to a few words, review it frequently, and refine it over time. Ideally, the concept will remain the same, but better words will punch it up.

Don't get stuck on this (or any) step. Put something on paper, and continue working on your SSP. Later steps will inform earlier ones. It's cyclical.

SSP Step 3: Core Values

Define the Core Values of your business (the things you care about). These are the values you want to instill in the people you lead. When it comes time to look for employees, you'll already know what you want. It doesn't matter how talented someone is at a task; if they don't believe in your company in the right way, they aren't the right fit.

You may want to categorize the Core Values as Internal (what you value for yourself or within your business) or External (your values toward and on behalf of your customers).

These values will also allow you to explore the right opportunities to collaborate with other businesses and vendors. Those you interact with will need to be in alignment with your values.

SSP Step 4: Vision Narrative

A vision defines what's possible. It should be in line with your mission statement and will provide guidance for the actions you will need to take over the next 3–5 years. It will change over time (as your vision grows or is achieved) but should be firm enough that it doesn't change daily.

Imagine walking through an ideal day 3–5 years in the future. Capture your environment and emotions. Detail what you do when you wake, how you interact with your family, and what tasks you work on. Include dreams you're working on for the future and how you wrap up your day.

Craft a vision for about one year from now and a vision for where you want to be three months from today. These shorter-term visions will point out the work required to attain the long-term vision. Use these as your plan becomes more tangible.

Your vision should be big enough to challenge you. Stand in awe of it, because once written, it's real and achievable. This process was inspired by an article Ari Weinzweig wrote for Inc. com called "Creating a Company Vision."

SSP Step 5: Business Objectives

List the specific things your business needs to accomplish. No more dreaming . . . these are future accomplishments!

Capture both professional and personal objectives. They will support each other in most cases.

Be specific and outline the overarching goals for your business . . . even if it may take decades to realize some of them. Imagine the impact of your business on your life as well as any impacts that may outlive you.

As a whole, your business objectives should cover five Key Results Areas. If one is missing, you've missed something important. The five KRAs are:

- **People:** Who are your clients, employees, vendors, family, etc., and how do you need to interact with them to grow your business?
- **Process:** What are your systems and tools, and what changes need to be made?
- **Profit:** How do you make money and plan to make more money?
- **Product:** What goods or services do you provide, need to provide, or need to eliminate?
- **Promotion:** How do you get the word out and let the world know you exist?

SSP Step 6: SWOT Analysis

Look over your initial SWOT Analysis and develop specific actions to leverage your Strengths, mitigate your Weaknesses, take advantage of your Opportunities, and eliminate your Threats. Copy the contents of your SWOT, and respond to each entry in detail.

SSP Step 7: Key Strategies

This is the part of the planning process where you narrow your focus and begin to prioritize your efforts. There will be more things to do than are possible. Put your energy into the most important things, and your business will have a fighting chance to survive and thrive.

Document your most important projects. Remember that a project has a specific purpose, an intended outcome, and a defined timeline. Structure your projects accordingly.

Once documented, the projects must be prioritized from the most important to least important. This is a subjective process, but objective criteria may be used to help (impact, precedence with other projects, profit, timing, available resources, etc.).

Must-Do Projects will get your immediate attention over the next 90 days, even if they may take longer to complete. These are the projects that typically have the biggest and most tangible Return on Investment (ROI), which can be more than just money.

Should-Do Projects are the holding pen for everything else you need to get done. Promote them as time or opportunities arise, but always act with intention. Some may never be realized, while others will be first in line for the next quarterly planning cycle.

SSP Step 8: Major Immediate Goals

Copy each Must-Do Project into the template and document the Major Immediate Goals for each one. Immediate is the key word. Planning too far out can be paralyzing. Instead, focus on the next 90 days and define the specific things you need to achieve to move your business forward.

Some of the projects will be completed within 90 days. Others will take longer. Document only goals that can be completed within 90 days. Create a sense of urgency and build momentum! Be aggressive but realistic in terms of resources (time, money, etc.).

SSP Step 9: Action Steps

Copy each Must-Do Project and Major Immediate Goal into the template. Then define the actions needed to accomplish each.

Every goal will have at least one action step (likely more). Set start and end dates, assign resources, and get to work!

When you first start this process, it's hard to know how long things will take and how much effort is involved. You will learn and adjust along the way.

The Planning Cycle

You can't know everything or have a perfect implementation. That doesn't mean you shouldn't plan. In fact, it means that it's more important than ever to have a plan. If you go through life without a plan, you'll probably end up accomplishing only accidental things.

By following a simple process, you can see how to give time to an effort in the face of resistance, as well as when it's time to make massive changes to your approach.

Planning is the first step and creates the foundation from which we will execute. But planning, doing, and adjusting misses a critical component: learning from our results. Therefore, we have to add a Review to the process. We need to evaluate our results and reevaluate our plans. What works and why? What doesn't work and why not? Has our vision shifted and are our actions still in line with the Vision Narrative? Has the market shifted, and do we need to shift with it?

This Plan-Do-Review-Adjust cycle is my take on the Plan-Do-Check-Act (PDCA) process developed in large part by Dr. W. Edwards Deming. To learn more, visit http://en.wikipedia.org/wiki/PDCA. It is a critical method that, when applied intentionally, will keep us on track and up to speed.

Quarterly Planning and Execution

The SSP prescribes a three-month planning period. This is a short enough time to manage at a detailed level, yet long enough to see if your plan is making progress or needs to be adjusted.

Plan for three months and **Do** the work. After three months, intentionally **Review** the results of your efforts. As you build the plan for the next three months, **Adjust** based on what you've learned.

Once per year, do a deeper review as part of your annual planning efforts. This is when bigger adjustments may be warranted, as well as when key parts of the plan may need updating (including the Vision Narrative—always keep it pushing into the future). Remember to build a Financial Forecast that aligns with your SSP.

Clarifying your purpose gives you power and direction. It gives you confidence to march forward. It gives you discernment to know whether you're on the right path or not. And it creates a vision not only for yourself, but for anyone joining you on the journey, from family and friends to employees and customers.

Go forth and do bold things!

Learn More

If you'd like to learn more about the SSP, check out these resources:

- The Book: *Conquer the Entrepreneur's Kryptonite*
- The Workbook: *Conquer Your Kryptonite Workbook*
- Contact me for personal training, speaking, or coaching at james@insignisinteractive.com.

Reasons to Align Personal and Organizational Purpose

Aligning personal and organizational purpose is important for today's leaders because it can increase motivation and engagement, improve decision-making and performance, enhance reputation and brand, and create positive social and environmental impact.

Here are more reasons why aligning personal and organizational purpose is important for today's leaders.

Attraction and retention of talent: Purposeful leaders who align their personal and organizational purpose are more likely to attract and retain talented employees who share their values and vision. This can help build a strong and diverse workforce committed to achieving the organization's goals.

Innovation and creativity: Aligned purposeful leaders are more likely to foster these qualities within their organization. Their clear and meaningful purpose inspires them to explore new ideas and solutions.

Resilience and adaptability: Leaders who align their personal and organizational goals are driven by a clear and meaningful purpose that helps them stay focused, stay the course, and overcome obstacles.

Customer loyalty: Purposeful leaders are more likely to build a loyal customer base.

Long-term sustainability: Purposeful leaders who align their personal and organizational purpose are more likely to build a sustainable organization. They are committed to creating positive social and environmental impact while also delivering value to their stakeholders and ensuring the organization's financial health and stability.

Wise leaders will work on aligning personal and organizational purpose.

Exercises

Create a vision board. Use images, quotes, and symbols that ignite inspiration and motivation to visually represent your personal vision and purpose.

Craft a personal mission statement. Concisely articulate your purpose, goals, and values, providing a guiding compass for your life.

Audit your purpose. Reflect on personal and organizational purpose, evaluating the alignment of actions with purpose.

Perform a stakeholder analysis. Understand and prioritize the needs, expectations, and values of those impacted by your work.

Conduct a competitive analysis. Compare your purpose with that of competitors, uncovering opportunities for differentiation and unique value creation.

Compose a compelling personal or organizational purpose statement. Capture your purpose, values, and vision as a guide.

Develop a purposeful action plan. Identify actions and goals aligned with your purpose and create a roadmap for their achievement.

Call to Action

Look over the steps in strategic planning, and then draft/sketch your plan.

Chapter 4: Setting a Vision

"A vision without a strategy remains an illusion."
—Lee Bolman,
Reframing Organizations: Artistry, Choice, and Leadership

Purposeful leaders play a vital role in guiding their organizations toward success by setting a clear vision and inspiring their teams to achieve it. This chapter explores vision-setting for purposeful leaders and the impact it has on organizational success.

Developing a compelling vision aligned with your business's purpose is critical to the success of any organization. A compelling vision is a clear, inspiring, and memorable description of the future you want to create and how you plan to achieve it. A vision statement should be aligned with your business's purpose, values, and goals, and it should inspire and motivate your employees, customers, and other stakeholders.

Make sure the vision is communicated in a way that resonates with the team and inspires them to work toward a common goal.

Here are some things your vision should be.

Aligned: Your vision should be aligned with your business's purpose, which is the reason why your organization exists. Reflect on your purpose and how it can inspire and guide your vision.

Engaging: Involve your employees, customers, and other stakeholders in the process of developing your vision. This can help ensure that your vision resonates with them and reflects their needs and expectations.

Ambitious: Your vision should be ambitious and aspirational and should stretch your organization to achieve more than it has before. It should motivate and excite your team and encourage them to strive for excellence.

Specific and measurable: Your vision should be specific and measurable, with clear targets and milestones that help you track your progress and stay focused on your goals.

Authentic and consistent: Your vision should be authentic and consistent with your business's purpose, values, and goals. It should reflect who you are as an organization and what you stand for and should be consistent with your actions and behaviors.

Once you have developed your vision, communicate it clearly and consistently to your team, customers, and stakeholders. Reinforce your vision through your actions and behaviors, and use it to guide your decision-making and priorities.

By doing this, you can inspire and motivate your team, differentiate your organization from competitors, and create a clear roadmap for success.

Crafting a Lasting Vision by Tad Dickel, PhD

The world is changing faster than ever before. Technology has allowed us to connect from almost anywhere, at any time, and instantly access information. Virtual meetings, remote work and on-demand services have become commonplace. But while some organizations have successfully adapted and thrived, others have buried their heads in the sand and failed. The difference has everything to do with planning and adapting.

Successful organizations need to create a long-term vision for the future and articulate it to stakeholders. Strategic planning is a process that helps any company or nonprofit analyze their purpose and articulate where they're going.

In *Strategic Planning for Public and Nonprofit Organizations: A guide to strengthening and sustaining organizational achievement*, John Bryson defines strategic planning "as a deliberative, disciplined approach to producing fundamental decisions and actions that shape and guide what an organization (or other entity) is, what it does, and why."

Strategic planning provides many benefits. Here are some.

Establishing a vision: What challenges need to be addressed and what opportunities need to be pursued? Strategic planning can help your organization develop an approach for both to put you on the right path to success.

Engaging people: Including employees, stakeholders and others in the process will help you garner support as you create a more sustainable vision. Survey others on their ideas, enlist focus groups and meet to discuss suggestions.

Communicating priorities: As you create a vision, you'll be better able to communicate organizational priorities internally and externally. Regularly share priorities and progress toward identified goals.

Enhancing mission: Strategic planning can help organizations clarify their purpose, which is very important for employees and stakeholders.

Despite all these advantages, some organizations still aren't engaged in strategic planning. I find there are three primary reasons for this:

1. **The focus is on day-to-day survival.** In *The 4 Disciplines of Execution: Achieving Your Wildly Important Goals*, keynote speaker Chris McChesney and his coauthors describe the "whirlwind" of daily responsibilities that consume all companies and employees. Daily demands and deadlines make it difficult to attend to long-term priorities.
2. **Leaders may not know how to do strategic planning.** They're unsure of how to design a process to develop a long-term vision and don't know how to create a plan format.
3. **Organizations struggle to find the right time.** There is no perfect time to begin planning. However, there may be less-opportune times, such as when a leadership transition looms, a company is undergoing major changes or in crisis, or during a busy season.

None of this is to say strategic planning of any kind is foolproof. Going through the planning process doesn't guarantee success, especially if it's done haphazardly.

Strategic planning processes can fail if any of the following occurs:

- **Leaders aren't committed to developing a plan and implementing it.** Success requires buy-in from the highest levels of an organization.

- **Goals are unclear.** Ambiguous or imprecise goals are the Achilles heel of many strategic plans. Strategic planning best practices include identifying measurable goals and timelines.
- **No plan exists for implementation.** Frequently organizations develop plans and think the work will just happen. Processes need to be established to regularly review and implement the plan.
- **Future plans are based entirely on past experiences.** Incremental change can be effective, but we also need to be bold in our thinking. The world has evolved, and we need to recognize that what we have done in the past may not work in the future.
- **Organizations try to do too much.** Strategic plans can grow beyond what is realistic to accomplish. Organizations set themselves up for success when they focus on doing a small number of things really well.

Core Planning Team

One of the most important aspects of a successful strategic planning process is assembling the right team to guide the effort. The chief executive (or board) has the ultimate authority but needs a dedicated team of people who will oversee the process.

I recommend organizations identify a core planning team with about eight members. It is tempting to make the executive team the default core planning team, but there is value in bringing together other team members.

The following are what team members should be:

- *Big-picture thinkers*: They should be able to see beyond the minutiae of daily work life to understand the major opportunities, issues and challenges that will affect the organization's future.
- *Open to diverse perspectives*: An inclusive team will have people from various areas of the organization, of different ages, genders and ethnic and racial backgrounds, some who are newer to the organization and others who have been there for a long time.

- *Able to set aside personal agendas:* They should be keenly focused on ideas that will best serve the organization as a whole, not beholden to personal interests.
- *Credible:* Many people in the organization might be skeptical of the planning process and resulting changes. That's all the more reason to find trusted individuals who have the best intentions of the organization in mind.

A champion or planning chair is typically needed to ensure the process goes smoothly. This should be a person who has proven leadership ability and credibility in the organization. Responsibilities may include convening and running meetings and driving the process forward.

The core planning team will need to meet on a regular basis, possibly over the course of several months. They will design the planning process, create the plan, and develop a system for implementing the plan.

Conceptual Agreement

You'll need to develop a conceptual agreement to outline what the strategic planning process will look like. That includes committing to reviewing the current state of the organization and being open to how things move forward.

The planning process should generally take one to three months to complete. If it takes too long, you'll lose momentum. If the period is too short, you may not be able to engage enough people or develop a plan with sufficient detail.

The core planning team should identify who will be involved with the planning process. Strategic planning is a fantastic opportunity for engagement, and as such, I recommend erring on the side of involving too many people. Get input through in-person or virtual listening sessions, surveys, town hall-style meetings and sharing plan drafts with stakeholders.

Using an External Consultant

As a strategy consultant, I am often asked whether a consultant is necessary to help lead the strategic planning process. I think it depends.

I see some organizations successfully navigate this process without a consultant. These organizations typically have staff who are skilled and experienced in strategic planning. In addition, the person who leads the planning process has the time necessary to keep things moving. On the other hand, some organizations choose to use a strategic planning consultant, and are happy with the outcome.

This segment has been written to empower and enable you to lead strategic planning without a consultant.

Your core planning team needs to discuss whether you have the capacity to lead the process on your own. You may decide to use an external consultant to help with portions of the process such as facilitating listening sessions, administering surveys, or leading meetings during the plan development phase. This hybrid approach can also be helpful and cost effective.

Communicating the Process to the Organization

Strategic planning should be approached as an exciting opportunity to assess the organization's current state, listen to one another, learn from each other, and become more focused on achieving your purpose. Stakeholders should know why the process is beginning and ways they may be able to get involved.

You'll first need to spend some time discussing the organization's purpose. Each organization has its unique characteristics and areas of focus that should be articulated in any vision or mission statement. If your organization already has a vision, mission statement or both, your core planning team should review those and make updates as necessary.

This may be a quick process if your purpose is already clear. If it's not, however, or there's a reason for changing your mission statement or vision, it may take longer.

Core Ideology

During the strategic planning process, it can be helpful for organizations to understand their core ideology. As defined by Collins and Porras in the October 1996 edition of *Harvard Business Review*, this reflects "the enduring character of an organization" and has two parts, core values, and core purpose.

"Core values are the essential and enduring tenets of an organization. A small set of guiding principles, core values require no external justification; they have intrinsic value and importance to those inside the organization."

"Core purpose ... is the organization's reason for being. An effective purpose reflects people's idealistic motivations for doing the company's work ... it captures the soul of the organization." The core purpose might be synonymous with what some organizations refer to as a vision or mission statement.

Your core planning team can decide whether the more conventional vision or mission statements or core ideology better describe your organization.

Reviewing Purpose Statements

For each organization, this process is different. Sometimes it's fast. Other times, not so much.

The quick review: I have worked with organizations that regularly review their vision or mission statements, and they find it accurately reflects who they are and want to be. This discussion can take less than 30 minutes.

A longer conversation: Some organizations have not reviewed their vision or mission statement in a long time. As a result, their core planning teams have decided the statements need to be reviewed and possibly modified. In these cases, I recommend discussing the following:

What do I like about the current statement(s)?

What do I not like about the statement(s)?

What is missing from the current statement(s)?

What makes us unique?

After an hour or so of talking all this over, it can be helpful to have someone on the core planning team craft a few new statements. These can be reviewed by the team at a future meeting. I have also had success asking each team member to come up with a version of a mission or vision statement and share it with the group. The group can discuss the different versions at another meeting. You might consider sharing the draft statements with members of the organization at listening sessions or employee meetings to get input.

Rather than agonizing over the perfect statement, focus on crafting one that reflects your organization, and which everyone can support and live out. Aim to complete it in one to three meetings.

Data Collection

An important aspect of strategic planning is assessing the current state of an organization.

The core planning team should identify the key data that are necessary for the planning process. I generally recommend compiling financial performance, staffing information, sales, major accomplishments and challenges, and any pertinent changes the organization has undergone.

This information can be compiled into a "State of the Organization" report to be shared with stakeholders.

Listening

It's important to get input from others in the organization and the community. While there are a number of ways to do this, the emphasis should be on listening and learning.

Strategic planning is a wonderful opportunity to engage internal and external stakeholders, so it's important to be thoughtful about who is included in the process.

Surveys

Many organizations can create and administer their own surveys, and these can be customized based on the type of feedback you're after.

You'll need to balance the length of time necessary to complete the survey with the depth of detail you desire. Shorter surveys will generally receive more responses, while longer surveys may limit participation but elicit responses that are richer in detail.

I recommend organization surveys include a SWOT analysis that asks respondents to identify the organization's internal Strengths, Weaknesses, external Opportunities and Threats.

Ask respondents to prioritize items from the survey that should be part of the strategic plan. Some organizations ask for demographic information and length of involvement with the organization. This data can help you decide if all demographic groups have been reached, though some people may not want to share this information, and that's okay, too. Online survey programs can also help break down responses by different demographics like age.

One limitation of surveys is that you're not able to ask people immediate follow-up questions to get more context for responses. But using surveys in combination with listening sessions can provide you with a more dynamic understanding of feedback.

Group Listening Sessions

I highly recommend using group listening sessions. These provide excellent feedback, and the facilitator can ask follow-up questions. You can accomplish a great deal in a two-hour listening session. The main downside is that some people may not feel comfortable sharing dissenting opinions with the group. In these instances, I encourage listening session attendees to provide this type of information in an anonymous survey.

For a listening session to be effective, it's important to find a strong facilitator to lead it. This person should be comfortable keeping the meeting on schedule, providing ground rules for the session, and encouraging all attendees to actively participate.

I find assembling homogenous groups can help people feel more comfortable sharing. Your organization might consider holding listening sessions with only employees from one department, people who are new to the organization, seasoned employees, or customers. We need to be aware of the power dynamics that keep people from fully sharing feedback. New employees might not feel comfortable opening up with long-time employees about their frustrations.

I'd generally suggest in-person listening sessions have no more than 20 participants and virtual sessions 12 or fewer to encourage participation. When groups are larger than that, you may have some people who don't contribute.

State of the Organization Presentation

This part is optional but strongly encouraged. Communication is a challenge in most organizations, and this event can be an opportunity to keep employees apprised.

I recommend a 10- to 15-minute presentation to communicate important information to attendees that improves their understanding of the strategic issues facing an organization.

The State of the Organization presentation can be delivered by members of the core planning team.

Facilitated SWOT Analysis

After the State of the Organization presentation, a facilitator should lead attendees through a SWOT analysis. At some organizations, executives and core planning team members stay to listen to participants, and at other companies, they feel like it's better to leave to ensure everyone feels comfortable sharing their opinions.

Before starting a SWOT analysis discussion, it's important to introduce some ground rules so attendees feel comfortable sharing. The facilitator might say, for instance:

"We are gathered today to discuss the future of our organization. I am going to ask you questions about the organization, and it is important that you be as honest as possible. We are not going to use this session to debate, judge, or evaluate your responses. If you think something, please say it, and I will write it down. At the end of the session, I will ask you to identify the most important priorities for the strategic plan."

The facilitated SWOT analysis asks attendees

1. What are the strengths of our organization?
2. What are our weaknesses?
3. What opportunities exist?
4. What threats do our organization face?

The strengths and weaknesses should typically focus on internal aspects of the organization, while the latter two questions are about external opportunities and threats.

Have the facilitator ask the questions. Then that person or someone else can record the answers. I recommend using an easel with flip chart paper and markers to jot down responses. You'll also need a room with plenty of wall space. Once you've filled up your sheet with responses, tear it off and hang it on the wall for everyone to see.

The facilitator should remain neutral and ensure others refrain from commenting on someone else's responses. If someone disagrees with a statement, the facilitator should remind the group that they're not judging or evaluating ideas. When applicable, the facilitator can take note of what a group member disagrees with to make sure people are heard and handle any conflict in a productive way.

After responses for each question have been captured, the facilitator should provide each attendee with stickers to select the responses that they feel are most important to include in the strategic plan. Color coding label stickers (small circular stickers) work well. I typically provide attendees with about five stickers each and give them 10 minutes to place their stickers on the responses they choose.

Once all attendees have done this, the facilitator can identify those responses that have a cluster of stickers. Thank everyone for their input, and let them know that the responses will be recorded and help the core planning team determine priorities for the strategic plan.

For transparency and as a follow-up, you might consider sending session attendees an email or letter with a copy of the typed responses.

Compiling the Report

At the end of the listening phase, all session notes and survey responses should be compiled in a single report. It can be valuable to organize the responses into themes and share the number of people who selected a response or theme as a priority. Any negative comments about individuals should be removed from the report.

If done correctly, the report will represent the experiences and feelings of stakeholders, and include their thoughts for the organization's future.

Developing the Plan

The vision and mission statement and data collected through the listening phase should guide decision-making as you start developing a strategic plan.

The next step will involve holding a retreat for the core planning team. This meeting will allow the group to reflect on responses and spend time together processing feedback and discussing priorities.

Core planning team members should receive listening session and survey reports ahead of time and spend time reviewing them. In-person retreats are preferred, but organizations may also consider virtual retreats to accommodate schedules and other constraints.

If your organization has not finalized your purpose statement(s), you should do this at the beginning of the retreat.

Reviewing Listening Reports

It's important for the core planning team to listen to and learn from feedback. We might have a tendency to be defensive, but it's critical to input. Someone should serve as a facilitator for the group and ask the following questions:

1. What are the reports telling you?
2. What surprised you about the responses?
3. How aligned are members of the organization with each other?

I recommend the facilitator write down all of the responses to these questions on large flip chart paper so everyone can see them.

Identifying Key Problems and Opportunities

In my work as a creative problem-solving facilitator, I've learned to define problems and opportunities through the phrase "How might we ...?" The phrase was mentioned by Dr. Min Basadur in an article that appeared in *Harvard Business Review* in September 2012. He explained:

"People may start out asking, 'How can we do this,' or 'How should we do that?' But as soon as you start using words like *can* and *should*, you're implying judgment: Can we really do it? And should we?" By substituting the word "might," he says, "you're able to defer judgment, which helps people to create options more freely, and opens up more possibilities" (para. 3).

This approach can be used to identify problems that need to be solved and opportunities to pursue. Many of the "How might we ..." questions will directly relate to the themes that emerged during the listening phase.

Once the group has made a good list of "How might we ..." questions, the facilitator should ask the core planning team to select approximately three to five of the questions that they think need to be addressed in the strategic plan.

The group should then discuss which questions might be a focus of the strategic plan. If some have similar themes, these can be combined.

After the selections have been made, the facilitator might also ask, "Do these questions address the strategic issues impacting our organization?" This is an important time to really reflect on key strategic issues, and it is ideal for the core planning team to reach a level of agreement.

I recommend having three to five questions to discuss and develop. Too many can lead to a lack of focus in a strategic plan.

Small Group Work

Once the group has narrowed down the number of questions, team members can break into small groups to discuss strategic focus areas.

The breakout groups should complete the following without agonizing over the details. Remember, this is a preliminary discussion to begin developing aspects of the strategic plan.

1. **Craft "How might we...?" questions.** Write in priority "How might we...?" questions that the core planning team selected.
2. **Select an "owner."** This is the person responsible for accomplishing the stated objectives. It's best to pick a person who will be responsible for implementing this part of the strategic plan. I caution groups against identifying committees as owners, since that often leads to a lack of follow-through and accountability.
3. **Pick team members.** Here you're identifying or creating a committee or team that will support the owner. Consider suggesting employees who could use their specific gifts and talents to help implement the strategic plan.
4. **Determine your desired outcome.** What do you really want to accomplish and how will you know you if you succeed? Begin with the end in mind and write a vivid description of the favored outcome. A paragraph is adequate.
5. **Create metrics.** For this you'll clearly articulate key measures for success in the first, second and third year,

and so on. This will help the organization work towards a specific goal.

6. **Outline your strategies and initiatives.** You'll be better equipped to meet metrics and achieve your desired outcomes in the first, second and third year. Consider the work required to accomplish your goals.

7. **Develop action steps.** Break down, into smaller bite-size pieces, the strategies and initiatives that you're planning for the first year of the plan.

8. **Outline the resources needed.** This may include budget dollars, staff resources or assistance from an external source. Although it can be difficult to estimate a cost, it is advantageous to provide as much information now as possible.

This exercise should take about 30 to 45 minutes. Once completed, the small groups will brief the full core planning team on their work. Allow time for comments, suggestions, questions and discussion. The recorder from each group can add in comments from the group on their worksheet.

Retreat Closing

At the end of the retreat, the next steps should be discussed. A member of the core planning team will need to draft an initial strategic plan based on the strategic planning worksheets. The plan may include:

1. **Owner:** as described above.
2. **Team:** as described above.
3. **Vivid description:** Develop a brief, precise description of what success in this focus area will look like.
4. **Outcome:** This will detail a 3–5-year goal. It should be measurable to the extent that's possible. For example, increase attendance from 300 to 400 people in 3 years.
5. **Metrics:** Break it into smaller, more manageable goals.
6. **Strategies:** Here you'll describe what you will do to achieve the goal over first, second and third years – and beyond. Instead of listing many different strategies, pick those that will have the most impact.
7. **Action steps:** as described above.

Communication

After the retreat, the core planning team will provide an update to the organization. Consider sharing the initial elements of the plan, asking for input and inviting people to get involved with its implementation.

You'll want to emphasize that the initial focus areas have been developed as a result of the feedback received from the organization and community. It's important to again thank everyone for their input and time. Then you might ask the following:

- Is there anything missing?
- What concerns do you have?
- What part of the plan would you like to help with?

The core planning team should meet to review any feedback received, identify volunteers who want to help and finalize the plan. This is also an important time to ensure support for the plan from the organization's leadership.

Although many organizations are initially intimidated by the prospect of creating a strategic plan, acting on it is the hard part. The rollout needs to include a strategy for communication and implementation, areas that are often neglected.

Communication Plan

A central function of any strategic plan is communicating a vision for the future. The core planning team should work together to develop a plan for articulating this vision.

The core planning team should identify stakeholders who will receive information about the strategic plan. There should be a meeting with employees to share the plan and to help them understand how they will be involved. Also consider communicating with the community at large through social media, the organization's website, bulletins, mass announcements and press releases and provide regular updates.

People appreciate hearing about progress, and this can include updates on successes, accomplishments, any changes to the plan, the need for help, and barriers to success.

Creating Focus Area Teams

To ensure the plan is implemented, it's critical to create focus area teams. These typically bring together six to eight members who possess applicable knowledge or experiences, and most importantly, are passionate about that focus area and committed to helping.

In an initial meeting, communicate the vision and strategic plan components and outline the expectations for focus area chairs and team members. Once established, focus area teams should — at least initially when the plan is first being implemented — meet every one to two months to offer support, problem solve and provide input.

Team members may be added as things progress or additional perspective is needed.

Implementation Plan

I often say that creating a plan is the easy part of strategic planning. Implementation is much more difficult. For that reason, the core planning team should prioritize determining how the organization will move forward with a strategic plan.

Once the implementation begins, I recommend the leadership team be responsible for overseeing the strategic plan. This team can also decide when it makes sense to provide updates, and make these a feature of regular meetings.

The strategic plan should be viewed as a living, breathing document. It's normal to adapt it as circumstances change.

A longer meeting can be held annually to review what's been accomplished in the last year and outline what needs to be done in the next year. This meeting might include members of the leadership and focus area teams.

Implementation Reports

At designated leadership team meetings, the focus area owner should provide a written update that indicates progress, next steps and challenges the team is facing.

The leadership team should discuss this focus area and affirm the desired outcomes, make suggestions or identify new resources.

Applying Lessons Learned in a Changing World

The world is changing faster than ever, so we need a strategic planning process that keeps up. My hope is that by now you feel knowledgeable enough to begin this process and make changes to the plan as needed.

For review, here are some things worth considering to put the lessons you've learned into practice:

- Strategic planning is a wonderful tool for engagement.
- Err on the side of involving too many in the process.
- Use this opportunity to clearly communicate your organization's vision and priorities.
- Whenever possible, make sure the goals you establish are measurable.
- It's easier to create a strategic plan than implement it – make sure you have a plan for the latter too.
- Encourage creativity and dream big.

This process is flexible and can be modified based on your organization's needs. Dennis Gabor said, "The best way to predict the future is to create it." Strategic planning helps us create the future we desire.

Chapter Recap

Setting a vision is an important part of your job, and strategic planning is a big component in setting that vision and staying on course.

Exercises

Ask yourself these questions. Write out your answers, and review them periodically. You might find that some of the answers change over time.

- What is the long-term vision for my business?
- What are the core values that guide my business?
- Who are my target customers, and what are their needs?
- What are the strengths, weaknesses, opportunities, and threats facing my business?
- What are the key success factors for my industry, and how can my business meet or exceed them?

- How can my business differentiate itself from competitors?
- What are the key performance indicators (KPIs) that I will use to measure success?
- How can I align my business goals with my personal values and purpose?
- What are the potential risks and challenges associated with my business strategy, and how can I mitigate them?
- How can I continually assess and adjust my business strategy based on changing circumstances and feedback from stakeholders?

Call to Action

Once you have communicated your vision and strategy to your team, follow up and reinforce your message on a regular basis. Provide updates on progress, and highlight successes.

Chapter 5: Building a Purposeful Culture

"Culture does not change because we desire to change it.
Culture changes when the organization is transformed—
the culture reflects the realities of people working
together every day."
—Frances Hesselbein, *Hesselbein on Leadership*

A purposeful culture can help your team members connect with the company mission and values as well as improve employee engagement, retention, and productivity. A strong purposeful culture can attract top talent and build a loyal customer base.

The Easy Button by Myhriah Young

Pushing the Easy Button for Culture with the DiSC Assessment Tool

Culture, culture, culture . . . There are buzzwords that make their way into the "business world," get thrown around for a while by marketing companies, and eventually become a part of our everyday language. It seems to me that "culture" is one of those, yet do company leaders really know what it means and how to implement it into their workplace?

So, what is culture, anyway?

The best definition I have heard over the last few years is this: Good company culture is what makes your employees not dread Mondays.

Many other definitions go much broader with it, such as this one from Darren Perucci's article, "What Is Culture [Plus 10 Expert Tips for Improvement]," found on Bamboohr.com: "It is a shared set of workplace beliefs, values, attitudes, standards, purposes and behaviors. It reflects both the written and unwritten rules that people in an organization follow."

It has been and still is a goal of mine to make this topic more tangible and less abstract or "pie in the sky."

How does someone go about creating a good company culture?

While there are no wrong ways to go accomplish this task, a large frustration that we have heard from employees when it comes to culture is that their leaders don't recognize that creating culture is not a cookie-cutter process and every company is going to be different.

You can use other companies as a source of inspiration; however, simply looking at what they are doing and trying to copy it clearly does not work.

Think about it like this: The Savannah Bananas have a great atmosphere they have cultivated over the years, and it is apparent in everything they do. From their very first interaction with their website to the invoice you receive when purchasing tickets, all the way to the entertainment at each game and their aftergame follow-up, they are very clear on who they are as a company — their culture. They have taken a lot of time to cultivate, challenge, and refine their atmosphere.

A CPA firm might be able to draw inspiration from them and of course follow their Fans First method (which I highly recommend, by the way). It would not make sense and would confuse everyone if the CEO suddenly decided they were going to take on the culture of this highly entertaining company. It would be wrong from the very first contact.

There are so many other wrong ways to create company culture, but I don't wish to outline those here. Instead, I would love to share a tool that can be very helpful in creating a workplace your team brags about.

Suppose the same firm decided not to use the cookie-cutter option or copy other popular companies. What if they wanted to tailor the atmosphere they planned to create based on the strengths of their company? How would they do that?

Enter the DiSC Personality & Behavior Assessment.

Now, before you start to tell me: "Oh, yeah, I took one of those at some job a long time ago. It wasn't that helpful. I think I was (insert D, i, S, or C here—most people don't remember)," please bear with me for a minute.

There are so many personality tests available. Why am I suggesting DiSC?

The modern, elegant, simple test can help create magic, especially when it comes to creating a culture around a growing company. The DiSC is a personality and behavior assessment that breaks up most human characteristics into four categories. We are all a little bit of each of them, and even though most people will be mainly one or two of those categories, we often borrow from the other characteristics based on our life situations.

We at the 48 Days DiSC Team have some terms and animals/birds we like to use to convey these four main categories:

D: Driven, eagle, or lion

i: Interactive, parrot, or otter

S: Steady, dove, or golden retriever

C: Creative (many call it Compliant or Conscientious), owl, or beaver

How do we bring this all together to create the Easy Button for culture as I promised in my title?

I'm so glad you asked. This is something I love to talk about.

There are many ways you can create a thriving workplace, but the main two that I've seen bring major changes are communication and motivation.

The first happens when leaders learn more about themselves. So often leaders are speaking in a completely different communication style than their team.

If we can help them understand their team, they can start to understand how to communicate in a way that helps team members to understand the goals and objectives. They can speak the same incentive language as their people, helping them to grow in a way that drives them to thrive.

Next, we help those leaders adapt their personalities and behaviors to fit the needs of their team around them, which opens their mind to see the natural way to structure how they can accomplish their tasks effectively.

Finally comes the pièce de rèsistance: Our Group Dynamics report. This is where The Creating Culture Magic comes in. We will get a snapshot of your team and a look at your shared ways, values, and goals.

While these aren't steps that immediately lead to creating a company culture, it is a great starting point to help the team work as a more cohesive unit, which will in turn begin to shape everything you do from who takes care of certain tasks and how you shape your customer experiences. You can use this knowledge to take care of everything from the website to the product or service you offer and how you interact with your community.

A Workplace Story

On Tuesday, our "eagle (D)" store manager attended her leadership meeting. She shared her numbers, which weren't as strong as many of her counterparts' in other areas. She then got the pep talk from her "eagle/parrot (i/D)" regional manager, who made it very clear that the numbers were not ideal—in the most upbeat manner, of course. The regional manager's contagious enthusiasm got the store manager excited. She knew if her team just "worked harder" and "pounded the pavement" more, she could get them excited about the changes and goals she was planning to implement. Then, at the next week's meeting, she would be able to "win" at the numbers!

Meanwhile, there were many larger issues happening to the store and its outside environment that were negatively affecting her staff:

- The area the store was in had become more dangerous with stores nearby being robbed on a regular basis.
- There was major construction around the area making it difficult for clients & staff to get to the store.
- They were drastically under-staffed, so customer service had greatly declined, and clients who came in were frustrated from the construction, lack of inventory, and the change the company had decided to make toward pushing for more online orders.
- There was a minor recession, so people were spending less and using less credit.

Our excited manager was ready to share her new ideas and goals with her team. She knew they were going to be just as motivated as she was. She came out and animatedly started telling her mostly "dove or peacemaker" team what they needed to do:

- "You need to get more clients to purchase, and make sure that you're asking every single client if they want to open a new card; if they hear the benefits, they will want one.
- Our numbers compared to last year are dismal; we must get those up. We're drastically behind where the company wants us to be.
- From now on, you need to make sure that one of you is always carrying the tablet for online purchases.

Change, change, change, goals, goals, goals, you, you, you..."

Are you also hearing the Charlie Brown "Wah-wah, wah-wah?"

Given the circumstances, much of her team was already feeling stressed and began to explain to her all the obstacles they were facing daily, many being things that no one could change. It knocked the wind out of the manager's sails. She ended up frustrated and started spouting off something to the tune of, "Well, we all just need to be happy to have jobs right now. You need to come and do the job you are being paid to do." She really felt like her team was sabotaging her and didn't like her at all.

How it Turned Around

What is to be done in this scenario? It can feel hopeless. How can it be fixed? We have seen this same thing in larger corporate settings when a CEO doesn't feel like their team is excited about company growth and their mission. We have also seen it in personal dynamics: a bride with her wedding party, a family who isn't communicating, even advisors at a college who feel like their students just need to graduate.

In this story, the manager had great intentions, and there wasn't much she could do to change the outside situations.

I am very happy to share that while it took some time, with DiSC training, they were able to start implementing changes that were helpful very quickly.

First, the manager took her DiSC assessment and learned that she tended to "bowl over" her team. She really wasn't used to listening to their needs or ideas. She just wanted them to get on board with what she wanted them to do. Barking orders out of her enthusiasm came across very differently than she intended.

Then she learned about her team. Most of them were S types (which is somewhat normal—69% of people are doves). She quickly implemented a very simple and impactful tip: the 7-second pause, so she could become a better listener. She found out they were actually great team players; they just needed her to help them understand the changes and give them some time to adjust, implement, and get set up for success.

Even though she couldn't change some of the larger problems, she heard what her team was saying:

- They had stayed because they were very loyal, but all of them were on the brink of a breakdown due to the difficult situations surrounding them. They liked her just fine as a person, not as a leader.
- Many of them struggled with the schedule because of the extra-long commute with the construction and were happy to come in but wanted her to understand that they needed their schedules to be worth it; 2-hour shifts were barely worth the gas.
- Her team was very willing to continue to do the things they needed to do to improve the numbers: upsell, ask about credit, wear the tablet for online orders, etc. However, they felt like she didn't "go to bat" for them. They wanted her to stick up for them and explain the situation and why they were having fewer clients in the store.

Listening took practice for our manager, and because of previous situations, her team wasn't quick to believe the change was permanent. However, she continued to put in the effort, and after a few weeks, her team really loved the changes they saw. It increased morale a great deal and created a safe space for more conversations about how to do more and get better numbers.

Trust takes time.

Roles Making the Difference

Now that the team was making improvements, they were able to implement another change very quickly: checking roles.

Our manager had an amazingly talented team. Most of them were not being utilized based on their strengths. Understanding this was where the true magic was. There were jobs that she needed done but had been doing them all by herself because of her lack of trust in her staff.

She was also being pressured to do more social media marketing and learned that she had a high "i" or parrot on her team who was aching to do that very thing. It didn't have to be added to the manager's gigantic list of things to do.

The most impactful thing that happened was her team took ownership. She was absolutely astounded. She had felt like she couldn't leave her team and still meet their goals. Her mentality was that if she didn't do it, it didn't get done. This was not the case at all. Her team was longing to be empowered to help her more. In fact, many of them knew how to do the tasks more efficiently than she did.

Our manager was not only able to delegate to the appropriate team members, but they started looking out for her, too. They did like her. They made sure she wasn't overworking, and she was able to take her first vacation in a very long time.

Results

This team continues to cultivate and create their culture, but these changes created an environment that allowed the work to begin.

This work helped them to tangibly see their shared values, ways of doing things, and goals. Often, the people we work with want to accomplish great things with us. They want to be a part of something bigger than themselves. They want to believe in the work that their company does.

If you can create a workplace that supports that, then the culture will begin to shape itself in a sense.

If you find yourself in a place where you're not sure how to get started, or you feel like your company has a culture "identity crisis," why not try working smarter rather than harder?

Why not give the DiSC Personality & Behavior Assessment? We love to help companies hit the Easy Button on company culture so that they can create their dream team.

You can work with us by checking out our website: www.48days.com/disc-assessments-for-business

From there, please feel free to schedule a call with me, the First Impressions Director of 48 Days. I would love to have a conversation with you. Whether you work with us or not, I have a plethora of resources to share that can help you on your journey, and I love to talk about all things culture and business related. Yes, I am a parrot, and I would love to talk to you!

Staff, Space, and Stories by Phil Mershon

Conveying Values and Developing a Shared Sense of Purpose and Meaning

How is culture defined? Edgar Schein, professor emeritus from Sloan School of Management at MIT, defines culture as "a pattern of shared basic assumptions learned by a group as it solved its problems of external adaptation and internal integration. . . . A product of joint learning."

Another definition of culture comes from Delise Simmons, Chief Culture Officer and Founder at The Culture Think Tank:

"Culture is a collection of the behaviors of the people in a team, group or organization."

A culture emerges whenever people form ongoing relationships where they do things together. For example, I know missionary kids who grew up in Papua New Guinea who created their own private language that they used just among siblings. Likewise, within a company, you'll find that different divisions and departments have their own unique subculture in terms

> Corporate culture is the only sustainable competitive advantage that is completely within the control of the business owner.
>
> —David Cummings, cofounder of Pardot

of how they work and relate. Effective leaders want to create a purposeful culture.

I'll never forget this greeting at the Customer Service Revolution put on by the DiJulius Group in Cleveland, Ohio, which showed their culture clearly. "Welcome, Mr. Mershon. We've been expecting you. Carisa here will escort you to your reserved seat. I hope you don't mind, but we gave you a seat right up front, so you can see everything that is going on. If you need anything at all, please don't hesitate to ask."

I decided to test them, so I asked for a lens cleaner. Check. Then I asked for a special kind of hot tea. They found something similar and had it to me in minutes. Check.

I was impressed by how attentive the staff was to my needs. They were constantly checking in on me, but it never seemed intrusive. I felt like a VIP, but as I watched, I realized they were making all seven hundred guests feel like VIPs.

They created a sense of shared meaning around treating every customer like a VIP.

These things impact your organization's culture substantially: staff, space, and stories.

Staff

Staff plays a crucial role in shaping culture. If your staff members are more focused on efficiency and process than they are on customer service, your clients and customers will feel that. Challenge your team to think at every step, *How will this affect the customer experience?*

Have you noticed the difference between the staff at Chick-fil-A and the staff at other fast-food restaurants? It's not their age. Almost all of these servers are teenagers or college students. The difference is in how friendly they are. Sometimes it becomes humorous to see how many times you can get them to say, "My pleasure."

A lead trainer at Chick-fil-A confided to me that they have very specific training guidelines for all new employees. While they do screen out those with an unfriendly disposition, all other skills are trained very intentionally.

We can do the same for our businesses. So, how do we do that?

Focus on your leaders. Everybody watches what the leaders say and do. If leaders reward certain behavior, you'll see more of that. If leaders ignore or tolerate certain behaviors, you'll also see more of that. Disciplining other kinds of behavior can make those stories become legendary. If a leader doesn't practice the values you profess, you'll find everyone else ignoring them, too. That's why a leader's first job is to *define* the values. Their second job is to *demonstrate* them consistently. Their final job is to *defend* them.

Exercise

Because staff starts with the leader, you need to examine your personal impact on your organization's culture. First, look at the culture you desire to create. Get honest feedback on how well you and your leadership exhibit the values, mission statement, and so on. Are there any obvious incongruencies? Which are the most detrimental if you don't fix them? Focus on those first.

Second, get people who know you well to answer this question: "Based on my behavior, what would you say are the most important things to me?" Ask a variety of people to answer this. Don't be afraid to ask your spouse and some close friends in addition to work colleagues, bosses, clients, and customers.

Never	Always
Point	Show them the way
Say "No"	Find a way to say "Yes"
Say "I don't know"	Find out the answer
Show frustration publicly	Be a duck
Pass by a problem	Stop, engage, and help solve the problem
Make excuses	Own it, even if it's not your fault
Gossip or complain	Remember you're always on stage
Deliver bad news via email	Make it right
Leave things to chance	Be prepared
Cold transfer	Warm transfer

Credit: Inspired by working with The Dijulius Group

As you look at these lists, identify where you can improve, but also celebrate places where your values match up with the culture you seek. We found that the "Never/Always" exercise from The

DiJulius Group is a powerful tool for deciding what behaviors you want to include and exclude from your organization's culture.

The chart demonstrates the ten pairs of behaviors they focus upon. You might find you want to replace some of these or adapt them to language that makes sense internally, but it's easy for anyone to grasp what you value.

Perhaps you can create something similar for your business.

Space

The way we use physical space has a dramatic impact on the culture we create. There are several considerations. Some of these you can control. Others you adapt to.

Space is also important in creating a culture with a shared sense of purpose and meaning. The physical environment, the layout, the design, and the ambiance all contribute to the culture. The way the space is used, such as having tables for team collaboration versus only one-person workstations, affects how people connect and collaborate. For example, open floor plans encourage collaboration and teamwork much more than cubicles do. Personalized workspaces and well-stocked break areas can boost employee morale and engagement.

At Social Media Marketing World, we learned to make intentional choices that reflect the fun, vibrant, energetic, and connection-focused culture we seek to foster. We started by adding tropical aromas to the air in the area where people check in. It's subtle, but we want people to feel relaxed and refreshed after a long day of traveling. We use live plants wherever possible, as opposed to artificial plants, because we want the air to feel fresh and alive. We use vibrant, beachy colors to keep the energy alive but keep enough elements that feel professional so people know that serious business can be conducted at our conference.

What about your work spaces or your Zoom backgrounds? What does your work environment say about who you are and what you value? Does it inspire creativity or promote efficiency?

Stories

Whether at a family gathering, a class reunion, or a large cultural event, communities find their identity through the stories they remember. Family members laugh about Uncle Jerry and the time he drank from the fish bowl. Grown men become like boys when they remember the stories and pranks from their college days. Nations remember their leaders, wars, and independence days.

In these ways, stories shape the history and language we use. But stories also have a way of predicting and defining behavior.

When I worked for Koch Industries, the stories were legendary of the executives who worked 60- and 70-hour weeks so they could be seen by the CEO when he left for the day. That inspired other younger executives to also work long hours.

Then there were the stories of people who got fired with no questions asked when they were caught looking at porn on company time and computers.

Stories zoomed around the company about the trader who lost a million dollars on a trade that went bad and instead of being fired, he was kept around because the leaders didn't want to waste that expensive lesson.

If you look at those examples, you can quickly discern a cultural pattern that employees seek to live within. Hard work is respected; the longer, the better. Don't cross certain moral lines. Don't be afraid to take risks as long as you keep learning.

Stories are a powerful tool for creating a purposeful culture. Shared stories help people connect, and they convey values and meaning. Leaders should share stories that reflect the organization's values, culture, and mission. Stories can be about how the company started, its mission, customer interactions, and successes and failures. These stories help to build a sense of purpose and meaning.

Chapter Recap

Building a purposeful culture requires using staff, space, and stories to convey values and develop a shared sense of purpose and meaning. Leaders must focus on defining the values, demonstrating them consistently, and defending them. They must also pay attention to the physical space and its impact on the culture, as well as share stories that reflect the organization's values and mission.

As a leader, you have the chance to influence the culture through the staff you hire, the space you create, and the stories you celebrate and rehearse. Intentionally choose the stories you want being told in and about your organization.

Exercises

Building a purposeful organization requires a culture that aligns with your values. You can take action consistently with that goal in mind.

Define purpose. Clarify your organization's purpose and values to align with your own.

Lead by example. Model the behaviors you want to see in your team.

Hire and develop for fit. Seek candidates who share your values and invest in their development.

Communicate and reinforce. Regularly communicate and reinforce your purpose and values.

Empower and recognize. Empower your team and recognize their contributions.

Continuously evaluate and improve. Regularly assess and improve your culture.

Creating a purposeful culture ensures motivated, engaged teams committed to your goals. #PurposefulCulture

Purposeful culture matters.

- Personal values alignment drives motivation and commitment.
- A sense of belonging fosters positive work environments.
- Clear expectations lead to purpose-driven focus.
- Consistent decision-making for effective outcomes.
- Attract and retain top talent with shared values.
- Build a purposeful culture for engaged teams and organizational success. #PurposefulCulture

Develop a shared purpose.

- Communicate purpose and values clearly.
- Involve employees in goal-setting.
- Foster collaboration and teamwork.
- Recognize and reward contributions.
- Provide growth opportunities.
- Listen to employee feedback.

- Developing shared purpose leads to motivated and committed teams. #SharedPurpose

Foster collaboration and cross-functional learning.

- Emphasize learning and development.
- Reward innovative ideas and contributions.
- Embrace change and adaptability.

Foster innovation and continuous improvement.

- Encourage creative thinking and risk-taking.
- Provide resources for innovation.
- Measure and track progress.
- Create long-term success and competitive advantage.

Call to Action

Collaborate with your stakeholders and put some thought into this because your purposeful culture may be the most important thing you build.

Chapter 6: Leading with Courage and Resilience

"A barve colonel makes a brave battalion."
—Frederick II, *Makers of Modern Strategy*

Courage and resilience enable leaders to navigate challenges and overcome obstacles in pursuit of their organization's purpose and goals.

Courage is important because it allows leaders to take bold and decisive action in the face of uncertainty and risk. It requires a willingness to step out of one's comfort zone, to challenge the status quo, and to stand up for what is right. Courageous leaders make difficult decisions, even if they are unpopular. They're willing to take calculated risks in order to achieve their organization's goals.

Resilience is also critical for purposeful leadership, as it enables leaders to bounce back from setbacks and failures and to maintain a positive attitude and outlook even in the face of adversity. Resilient leaders persevere through difficult times and maintain their focus and commitment to their organization's purpose and goals, even when things are not going according to plan. An example of that is when conflict arises.

Navigating Conflict by Ron Price, MA

Conflict—what a scary word! I saw a survey once that said 67% of Americans say they dread conflict. I think at least some of the other 33% lied. But that may explain why so many people try to avoid conflict at all costs. While avoiding conflict may be common, it is a mistake on two levels.

For one, you simply cannot avoid conflict. As an imperfect human being who regularly interacts with other imperfect human beings, you will encounter conflict from time to time. You may experience even more than most simply because of your leadership position. Conflict is a normal component of life and does not necessarily mean you cannot continue to work with or engage with the other person just because the two of you disagree now and then.

My second reason why you should not try to avoid conflict is that doing so typically makes a situation worse, not better. If the matter is trivial and you really can ignore it altogether, then avoiding it might be appropriate. Unfortunately, that is not usually the case. Most people try to avoid conflict for fear of a negative outcome should they try to discuss the matter with the other person. They try to stuff their true feelings, but they likely will come out at some point and quite possibly in a negative, destructive way.

One possible explanation for why so many of us have an aversion to conflict is that we have had negative experiences which led to a loss of a relationship or an opportunity of some sort or, in some way, caused us pain. While those memories are real, I dare say that while conflict may be inevitable, damaged relationships, poor morale, and low productivity are all optional. That is if, and it's a big if – if you handle the conflict productively.

Prevention and Resolution

Rather than trying to avoid conflict, you would be far better served to prevent it when possible and to resolve it productively when that is the more appropriate option. By preventing conflict, I'm referring to the minor, trivial matters that, if you are not careful, can grow exponentially into a situation you do not need, want, or deserve. Of course, not all conflicts can or should be prevented, but many can. Think back to when you went to bed angry about something and awoke the following day wondering what the big deal was. Or perhaps a situation with a direct report did not go well but was nearly forgotten the next day, if not later that same day.

A helpful tip in preventing conflict is to remember that you and everyone you interact with have a deep-seated desire—make that need—to be understood. Not by the casual acquaintance perhaps, but certainly by those who play a significant role in your day-to-day existence. This need to be understood starts early in life. Shortly after birth, babies cry to express their needs hoping that someone will recognize and satisfy them. Then we reach the toddler stage and gain some usage—I almost said mastery—of the language. Have you ever been around a toddler who is trying to be understood, but no one understands what they are saying? That is certainly not a pleasurable experience for anyone involved.

This need to be understood grew as you entered grade school and onward as you began interacting with teachers and fellow students, and it continues with you today. Many conflicts occur because both parties are trying to be understood at the same time. So they are both talking, and nobody is listening. If nobody listens, it follows then that nobody addresses the issues between them. The conflict continues. I heard that referred to as the "Shoot 'n' Reload" method of communication, which is very ineffective and damaging to productive relationships.

In the Covey Seven Habits of Highly Effective People program, Habit Five is "Seek first to understand, then to be understood." I honestly feel I would not have had a 30+ year career as a mediator if people had followed this advice. If you realize the other person or persons you are dealing with want and need to be understood by you, why not give that to them? If you value the relationship, is that too much to ask? Certainly, as a leader, you have a right also to be understood by them, but what do you have to lose by letting them go first? I suggest you have little or nothing to lose but much to gain. By demonstrating a willingness to understand them, you place yourself in a far better position for them to do the same for you.

Helpful Practices

A helpful practice in helping others feel understood is implementing four powerful words. When someone attempts to help you see their perspective on something, gently say, "Tell me more, please." You invest in your relationship with them by giving someone the gift of truly listening to them with an earnest desire to understand them. You also go a long way to being a leader people want to follow, and you increase your ability to navigate future conflicts you might face.

One of my favorite tips regarding successfully navigating conflict is the practice of calling a time-out the correct way. Far too often, people call a time-out the wrong way, and that typically makes a situation worse, not better. However, calling a time-out the correct way most often results in a productive conversation and improves the odds for a successful resolution to conflict.

Imagine for a moment people engaged in a conversation that is getting heated and ugly. Often, one person will throw up their hands and angrily say time-out as they exit the conversation. That puts an end to the negative interaction, but it leaves the other party with uneasy questions. If you just storm out of such a conversation, the other is left to wonder if you are ever coming back, if they will ever have the chance to converse with you, or if you are walking out of the relationship altogether.

Chances are you are simply trying to avoid an ugly encounter and don't want to say or do something you might regret later. While that is fine and proper motivation, you owe it to the other person to inform them of your intent. All you have to do is tell the person that you are too upset to speak at the moment but that you will come back at a specified time when both are in a better frame of mind to converse effectively.

So, the correct way to call a time-out is to schedule the time-in. Doing so lets them know you are not rejecting them or the relationship, and you will give them a chance to be understood, typically within 24 hours. This gives both parties a chance to calm down and later speak *with* each other, not *at* each other.

No one ever said leadership would or should be easy. And if anyone ever told you it would be free of conflict, they likely lied to you about other matters as well. But it is within your ability to prevent many disputes and resolve others in a lasting, mutually acceptable manner. Easy or not, I think you will find it is worth the effort.

You can gain more knowledge and skill in CPR (Conflict Prevention & Resolution) in my *PLAY NICE in Your Sandbox* book series or my CPR Mastery video course. See my website, ronprice. com, or email me at ron@ronprice.com for more information.

Steps to Navigate Conflict

A purposeful leader can navigate conflict by following these steps.

Stay calm. It is important to remain calm and composed during conflict to maintain a rational perspective and prevent the situation from escalating.

Listen actively. A purposeful leader must listen actively to all parties involved in the conflict to understand their perspectives and identify the root cause of the problem.

Seek to understand. Once the leader has gathered all the necessary information, they should try to understand the concerns and emotions of each party.

Communicate effectively. The leader should communicate effectively, clearly and respectfully to convey their understanding of the situation and their proposed solution.

Find common ground. A purposeful leader should work towards finding common ground between the parties involved to reach a resolution that benefits everyone.

Implement and follow up. The leader should implement the agreed-upon solution and follow up to ensure that the issue has been resolved to the satisfaction of all parties.

Learn from the conflict. After the conflict has been resolved, the leader should reflect on the situation and identify any areas where they could have handled the conflict differently to prevent similar conflicts in the future.

Courage and resilience help leaders to stay committed to their organization's purpose and goals even when faced with significant challenges or setbacks. By demonstrating these traits, leaders can inspire their team members to persevere through difficult times and to stay focused on the organization's mission and vision. This can help to create a culture of resilience and perseverance, which can ultimately lead to greater success and achievement for the organization as a whole.

Overcoming Challenges and Setbacks

Here are some ways to overcome challenges and setbacks:

- Cultivate a growth mindset as advocated for by Carol Dweck in her book, *Mindset*.
- View challenges and setbacks as opportunities for learning and growth.
- Stay flexible.
- Seek support.

- Learn from failures. Reflect on past experiences, analyze areas for improvement, and develop a plan for addressing them.
- Role-play scenarios. and visualize success to build your confidence and resilience.

These practices help you remain aligned with your purpose and values even in difficult situations.

Empowering and Developing Your Team

Empowerment and development are critical components of purposeful leadership. As a purposeful leader, it is your responsibility to create a supportive environment where your team members can thrive and grow.

Empowering your team members means giving them the tools, resources, and autonomy they need to make decisions and take action. This can help build trust and increase motivation, as team members feel valued and respected. When team members feel empowered, they are more likely to take ownership of their work, and contribute to the organization's overall success.

One area you should be sure to empower your people in is work–life balance.

Work–Life Balance

Fostering work–life balance is an essential aspect of purposeful leadership. As a leader, it is important to prioritize your own well-being and model healthy habits for your team. This means finding a balance between work and personal life that allows you to be fully present and engaged in both areas.

Purposeful leaders understand the importance of creating a workplace culture that supports work–life balance. This includes providing flexible work arrangements, promoting self-care, and encouraging employees to take time off when needed. By prioritizing a healthy distribution of time and energy, purposeful leaders can help reduce burnout and increase productivity, job satisfaction, and retention rates among their team.

To achieve work–life balance, purposeful leaders can use a variety of strategies, such as setting clear boundaries between work and personal time, delegating tasks effectively, and practicing self-care activities like exercise, meditation, or spending time with loved ones. It is important to recognize that balance will look different for everyone and to prioritize what works best for your own individual needs and circumstances.

Work–life balance is an essential aspect of purposeful leadership that contributes to the overall well-being and success of both the leader and their team. Here are some ways you can support this.

Show empathy. Recognize that your team members are people with personal lives, and empathize with their struggles. Show compassion and be willing to listen.

Offer flexibility. Consider offering flexible work hours or allowing your team members to work from home to help them balance their work and personal responsibilities.

Provide resources. Connect your people with resources such as an employee assistance program or counseling services.

Check in regularly. See how they are doing, and offer support as needed.

Maintain confidentiality. Respect your team members' privacy and keep their personal information confidential. This can help them feel safe and supported.

A Variety of Worlds

Not everyone hails from the same socioeconomic class, and you may need to learn to "speak someone's language" to connect well with and empower them. By embracing your role as a catalyst for change and creating a culture of empowerment, you can unlock the potential within your team members and inspire them to embrace their unique strengths despite the struggles they face.

Let's look at a transformative journey of leadership, where the empowerment of others becomes the cornerstone of a purposeful vision. The following is the story of Cosette Leary, motivational speaker, transformational coach to the impoverished, and author of *From Welfare to the White House*.

Arrange whatever pieces come your way.
—Virginia Woolf

Transforming My Life by Cosette Leary

Embracing Authenticity and Empowering Others

I came from another world. In the desolate landscape of my life of poverty, I found myself trapped in a cycle of stress, feeling like a cliché: a single mom struggling to make ends meet.

Every day was a blur of crisis and confusion, weighed down by the heavy burden of anxiety and trauma. I yearned for a fresh start, a do-over, to escape the confines of my limited existence and embrace a life of purpose.

> Your purpose as a leader is not just to achieve success but to inspire and empower others to reach their full potential.

Envy

The lives of others, filled with joy and abundance, became a source of envy as I witnessed families embark on exciting vacations and children decked out in trendy clothes. Meanwhile, I could only stalk my mailbox, hoping to find discounted tickets to the local zoo.

Yes, I wanted to be like the beautiful people I saw on TV. I wanted success, happiness, and a star-studded, crystal-white, pearly smile.

A sense of belonging is another thing I craved. I longed to be an active participant in society rather than a passive observer relying on social-service programs to get by. Their amplified echo blared over the welfare office's bullhorn: "Number A52 to window E . . ."

The life I longed for would not include the degrading shame tangled up in circumstances such as frequently overdrawn checking accounts, insufficient money to cover the bills. Neither would it include embarrassment over buying food with paper food stamps, which over the decades, would become the plastic EBT food stamp card of the SNAP program.

There was a real problem with my wishing for a well-rounded life. A severe speed bump crossed my road to obtaining that voluptuous do-over.

To embark on the journey toward a more fulfilling life, I needed to begin a profound process of self-discovery. I had to confront the depths of who I was and what I truly desired. Through introspection, I unearthed the real me—the person yearning for a life filled with celebration, security, and the chance to utilize my unique talents to make a difference. I longed for dignity, respect, and the opportunity to uplift others. With newfound clarity, I proclaimed my true identity to the world, ready to reclaim my life.

Ownership

But it required more than mere recognition; it demanded taking full ownership of my circumstances and abandoning the habit of blaming the world for my problems. I had to recalibrate my compass and chart a new course, guided by self-respect and an unwavering belief in my potential.

This transformation meant setting internal boundaries against negative self-talk, refusing to succumb to fear or self-doubt. I started embracing my strengths, celebrating my existence, and venturing beyond the confines of my comfort zone.

Discovery

The path to personal growth was fraught with unexpected challenges. As I worked to bridge the gap between social classes and merge my inner-city upbringing with middle-class norms so prevalent in corporate environments, I encountered the illusions perpetuated by society. People often presented carefully curated facades, projecting confidence and success while privately grappling with insecurities and breakdowns.

I had naively attempted to emulate their lives only to discover that their experiences couldn't truly align with my own. It became evident that I needed to find my own vocabulary, authentic to my journey, and not succumb to the external pressures imposed by societal norms.

Despite my impressive accomplishments and prestigious internships, I faced a harsh reality when I found myself back at ground zero, homeless and struggling to secure a job that matched my qualifications. The paradox was baffling, shattering my pride and leaving me disoriented.

Transformation

It was in that moment of despair and introspection that a transformative shift occurred. I no longer sought to impress or conform. Instead, I embraced humility and reflected upon the essence of my existence. My true calling was to be an agent of change, a beacon of motivation, guiding others toward a better life. Purposeful leadership was my path.

The realization was profound—I was unique, an individual with immense power and potential. It was this understanding that fueled my determination to break free from the shackles of society's expectations. I embarked on a mission to empower others, to help them recognize their own worth and unlock their true potential. On this grand stage of life, we each have a role to play, and it is up to us to seize the spotlight and make our mark.

I am still learning middle-class norms. I'm still learning how to speak your language. Can you speak mine? I don't understand some of the words you use, but I want to be able to live through my passion, which is to empower other people and elevate myself.

Proposal

Today, I challenge you to take a step back, even if it means stumbling and falling, for it is in moments of vulnerability that we truly discover ourselves.

Embrace your individuality. Harness your unique strengths. Then embark on your journey to make a lasting impact as a purposeful leader.

Realize that some of your people come from the same struggle I did. Help them navigate your environment. The time to start is now—run with unwavering determination, and claim your place in this world.

As a purposeful leader, you have the ability to unlock the hidden talents and potential within your team members, fostering growth and continuous development.

Development

Developing your team members means helping them learn and grow, both personally and professionally. This can include training, coaching, mentorship, and other forms of support. When team members have opportunities to develop their skills and knowledge, they are more likely to feel engaged and fulfilled in their work, which is one of the main things employees look for in a job, according to several sources, including Gallup.

Overall, empowerment and development help to build a purposeful organization that values its team members and is committed to their growth and success. By prioritizing these elements, purposeful leaders can create a supportive environment. that fosters engagement, motivation, and long-term success.

Delegation

Effective delegation is important to purposeful leaders for several reasons. It allows leaders to focus on their core responsibilities. Delegating tasks to others frees up time for leaders to focus on strategic and high-priority tasks that align with the organization's purpose and goals.

By delegating tasks to team members, leaders can help them develop new skills, gain experience, and grow in their roles.

Delegating tasks and responsibilities demonstrates trust in team members and promotes collaboration, as it encourages them to work together and share knowledge and skills.

Delegating tasks to team members who have the right skills and expertise can help improve efficiency and productivity, as it allows tasks to be completed more quickly and effectively.

It also can improve decision-making. Delegating responsibilities to team members encourages them to take ownership of their work and make more decisions, which can improve decision-making and problem-solving skills.

Overall, effective delegation is an essential skill for purposeful leaders as it enables them to lead their team effectively, develop team members, build trust and collaboration, and achieve their organization's goals efficiently and effectively.

5 Techniques for Delegating Effectively

1. Choose the right person for the task.
2. Communicate clearly regarding the expectations, timeline, and outcome.
3. Provide the necessary authority, resources, feedback, and recognition.
4. Monitor progress while giving autonomy.
5. Learn to let go.

By using these techniques, purposeful leaders can delegate effectively and help their team members grow and develop.

Providing Effective Feedback and Coaching

Providing feedback and coaching is an essential aspect of supporting a team's growth and development, as it helps team members improve their performance, learn new skills, and achieve their goals. Purposeful leaders understand that regular feedback and coaching are critical to promoting individual and team development and building a culture of continuous improvement.

Provide timely feedback. Purposeful leaders provide feedback in a timely manner, so team members have an opportunity to reflect on their performance and make improvements.

Be specific. Effective feedback is specific and focuses on behaviors that can be changed. Purposeful leaders provide specific feedback that is actionable and helps team members improve their performance.

Use the right communication style. Different team members respond to different communication styles. Purposeful leaders tailor their communication style to the individual and provide feedback and coaching in a way that is most effective for each team member.

Set goals and objectives. Purposeful leaders set clear goals and objectives for their team members and provide feedback and coaching that supports their progress toward these goals.

Encourage growth and development. Purposeful leaders encourage their team members to grow and develop by providing opportunities for learning and development and supporting their career aspirations.

Overall, providing feedback and coaching is an essential aspect of purposeful leadership, as it supports individual and team development, promotes a culture of continuous improvement, and helps achieve organizational goals.

Chapter Recap

Courage and resilience are indispensable qualities for purposeful leadership, as they empower leaders to navigate adversities and surmount barriers while pursuing their organization's purpose and objectives.

Exercises

- Conduct one-on-one meetings with team members to build trust and communication.
- Set SMART (Specific, Measurable, Achievable, Relevant, and Time-bound) goals with each team member to align individual objectives with team goals. Ken Carfagno, host of the *Smart Cleaning School* podcast, is an expert on helping leaders and teams set SMART goals.
- Conduct regular performance reviews and provide constructive feedback to help team members improve their performance.
- Encourage continuous learning and development by offering training and development opportunities.
- Recognize and reward team members for their accomplishments and contributions.
- Foster a positive work environment by encouraging collaboration, creativity, and innovation.
- Build a sense of community and belonging by organizing team-building activities and social events.
- Encourage open and honest communication by creating a safe and respectful work environment.
- Foster a culture of diversity and inclusion by celebrating differences and promoting equity and fairness.

Call to Action

Look for and create three opportunities this week for team members to take on leadership roles and responsibilities.

Chapter 7: Measuring Success and Making an Impact

"Success is not the key to happiness. Happiness is the key to success. If you love what you are doing, you will be successful."
—Albert Schweitzer, *The Spiritual Wisdom of Albert Schweitzer: A Selection from His Writings*

How do you measure success? Is it visible, such as a high salary, vacations, and other perks? Perhaps it is more about the satisfaction and impact. In this chapter, we're going to consider the different ways to measure success and make an impact. Let's start with how generosity feeds your success.

Network and Generosity by Kent Sanders

No matter where you work or which role you have, a powerful network is critical to your success. But how can you connect with people in a way that is genuine and doesn't stress you out? You learn the incredible power of generosity to help you build relationships with people in a natural way that is easier and far more fun than you ever thought possible.

Two Core Values: People and Generosity

One of the most critical things we have to remember is that it's not ultimately about the work we produce. Yes, that's part of it, but great work without great relationships and connections is not worth that much.

On the other hand, you can be just so-so at the technical aspects of what you do, but if you have amazing connections and a great network, wonderful things can happen. It's not just about the work—it's about the people.

That brings us to building a valuable network through the power of generosity. Let's define some terms.

Valuable network: A network is simply the people you know and who know you. It goes back to the fact that people do business with those they know, like, and trust. A valuable network is a growing collection of relationships that add more value to you and them over time.

Generosity: This is a life orientation toward giving. There are many reasons to look at life this way. Personally, I think it's more fun to give and be generous. It's also a much more effective way to build relationships and bring good things into your life than if you're stingy or hold back.

I believe we are to be stewards of what God has given us. You don't really own anything. Everything is just on loan. Looking at life this way makes giving a lot easier. It means you wake up every day asking, "What can I give? How can I help someone today?"

I operate on the conviction that anyone can build a powerful network, and anyone can be generous. It has nothing to do with talent. Even introverts can do all of these.

Focusing on growing my network has paid off in a lot of different ways the last few years. Hosting a podcast has played a huge role in this as well.

I want to share with you five key ways to grow your network by being generous. Every purposeful leader can do this.

1. Make referrals and introductions. You have friends who do certain types of work. When we hear of someone who needs that thing done, then we refer our friend. This is important because we like to do business with people we know, like, and trust. If we make a referral, we are passing on that trust to the person we are referring. So the person being referred comes to the potential client with some trust already in their pocket, assuming the relationship we have with the potential client is good.

I refer people all the time. It's fun and easy. All three people win when you make a good referral. The person you are referring gets potential business, the person you're referring them to gets someone they trust, and you win because now both people trust you even more, plus you have done some good in the world. And it might come back to you interesting ways in the future.

The same is true for introductions between people. I am constantly introducing people who need to know each other. Amazing things can come of this!

Don't overthink it. As you go about your day, pay attention to conversations and ask yourself, "Who does this person need to know?"

2. Write reviews for books and podcasts. Remember: people's #1 need is to feel affirmed and valued. A great way to do this is to leave a review for someone's podcast on iTunes, or leave a review for their book on Amazon and Goodreads. Then take a screenshot of your review and send it to the person, or better yet, post it on social media and tag the person. Simple and easy. (Pro tip: Leave your name and title at the end of reviews for a little extra PR boost.)

3. Send gifts and handwritten cards to people. I do this all the time for my podcast guests and many others whom I want to thank for any reason. Now, sending a card does take some time and a little bit of money because there's postage, but the return you get is amazing. People really love getting stuff in the mail that isn't bills.

Oftentimes, I also include a little key in the card—a skeleton key. I write something like "This is a little reminder of your power to unlock other people's creative potential." People go nuts for it; they really do. We all love trinkets and little reminders of important truths.

I also send out books to people. I just sent out a bunch of books to podcast guests a few weeks ago. One of the benefits of doing this is that people sometimes post a picture of the book on social media. I don't do it to get the pics, but it's great marketing.

There are all kinds of other gifts you can send as well. Check out John Ruhlin's book *Giftology* for great ideas.

Sending cards and gifts might seem like a hassle, but that's precisely why you should do it: hardly anybody else is doing it. You will stand out.

4. Send personalized videos. Here's something I learned from my friend Aaron Hunt, who is a personal branding expert. He is a master at sending short, personalized videos to people. So is my friend Andy Storch.

When you want to forge a deeper connection with someone, use an app like Loom to record a short video, saying something about what you appreciate about the person, or what you noticed, or some kind of mutual connection you have. Then make sure to title it with their name: Video for Steven, etc. That way it shows up as a personalized video. Be sure to make it short, just a minute or two.

This is how I got my second ghostwriting book. I sent a personalized video to the person just to say what I appreciated about their work and how it impacted me. That led to a phone call to connect, and the rest is history.

If you are an introvert, you probably don't like video, and it's not my medium of choice, either. But it's just like sending handwritten cards: hardly anybody does it. It's powerful and effective because it's rare. I would challenge you to get comfortable on video. Learn to make it your friend. People don't care if you come across as perfectly smooth. The fact that it's from you, and is authentic, is what makes it so powerful.

This strategy is immensely powerful. If there's only thing you do from this list, pick this one.

5. Be a guest on other people's podcasts. This requires time and some strategy but can yield substantial results. When you are a guest on a show, it can exponentially expand your reach because you're essentially borrowing someone's platform and audience. Here are a few things to keep in mind.

Find shows that clearly match your area of expertise.

When you pitch yourself to the people running the show, you have to demonstrate that you can add value to the host's audience. One huge mistake people make is not listening to the show beforehand, so their pitch is off.

If you do it the right way, this can be an awesome strategy for building your network.

Two Objections

Objection #1: I don't have the time to mess with all this networking stuff.

Yes, it can be time-consuming. But relationships are the most important thing you have in life. And the very reason you must do it is because so few people are putting the time into it. There is virtually no competition because most people are not willing to do the hard work of building a great network over time.

Objection #2: Why do I have to mess with all this? Why can't I just focus on my work?

The reason is because it's not just about your work. It's who you know and who knows you. This is the way the world has always worked.

Just work on it a little at a time. You will get used to it. The more you do, you more comfortable you will get. Remember that it's all about people.

What is one thing you can do today to be generous and build your network?

Tracking Progress

It is essential to track progress and determine whether you are achieving your goals and fulfilling your purpose.

Define your metrics. What will you use to measure your success and impact? Choose metrics that are specific, measurable, and aligned with your goals and purpose.

Monitor progress. Track to stay on target. You might want to use regular check-ins or performance reviews.

Examine results. Evaluate at preset intervals. Are you achieving your goals and making a positive impact? Adjust your strategy as needed.

Ask for feedback. Talk to your team, customers, and stakeholders. Do they think you are leading well and making a positive impact?

Celebrate successes. Acknowledge everyone's successes along the way to keep your team motivated and engaged. This will help build momentum and inspire continued progress.

A purposeful leader can measure success and make an impact by setting and tracking key performance indicators (KPIs) that align with their organization's purpose and values.

By doing these things, you can ensure that you are fulfilling your purpose and making a positive difference in the world.

Network generously.

Sales as a KPI

One important indicator of how a business or other organization is doing is sales. Even nonprofits make sales of one kind or another. Getting a grant approved and convincing a patron to use your services are both sales.

Teaching Yourself Sales by John Buchy

If you are in leadership of any kind, even just as the head of your household, you are in sales. You are trying to influence someone in their best interests to help serve that person. Your leadership helps them to get what they want and you to achieve goals for your organization, whether it be an employer, charity, or family.

One of the best practices is to develop good listening skills. You want to work on and get better at your communication skills. The best communicators are often the best "salespeople." Look for ways to ask the best questions, so that you can understand the goals of the people you are serving. Look for ways that you can help with their solutions. The more you show that you want to help them, the easier it is for them to want to do business with you. It helps you build your influence with them.

Being Likable

Work on having a positive mental attitude, and convey that you are an amiable person who is enjoyable to do business with and interact with. We all want to do business with people that we know, like, and trust. Anything we can do to build trust and likability is a good thing to pursue. To be successful in sales of any kind, you want to build the best relationships you can with the people you are serving.

To paraphrase Jim Cockrum, "God created a business so that people would have to build relationships with each other." The way I look at it is if the business is biblical, then you want to follow the Ten Commandments. For ease, you want to follow the Golden Rule and treat people how you want to be treated. If you do this, you're probably going to do very well in life.

You want to get in the habit of being easy to do business with and likable.

Building Trust

If you build good relationships with your customers, it is easy to build trust. It's more enjoyable for them to do business with you, and that leads to great deals for you, the customer, and the company or entity that you work for.

Walking away after a business deal or transaction knowing that everyone had their best interest in mind is a good feeling. Your customer will appreciate you working for their best interest, and a lot of times they will tell their friends, family, and even acquaintances about how well you worked with them and treated them. That is the best kind of advertising you can have: third-person credibility from an advocate of you. To get to that point, you have to build a good relationship with the customer.

Always be looking for ways to build better relationships with your customers. That way, when a competitor approaches them, they say, "We are happy doing business with the companies we already do business with."

By being a reader of a leadership book, you already have an advantage over quite a few salespeople. You are already working on one of the most important things that you can do in sales: self-education.

Self-Educating

Continuous learning in how to build our communication skills and influence is the best way to grow sales and serve the people we are trying to help as best we can.

Listen to sales books and podcasts on your phone as you're driving around, or mowing the grass, or exercising. As Zig Ziglar would say, become a member of "Automobile University." Even if you only do it a little bit a day, it will help grow your skills. Personally, all I listen to as I drive around are self-development business and sales kinds of books, YouTube videos, and podcasts. One of my favorite quotations from Jim Rohn is, "Formal education will earn you a living; Self-Education will earn you a fortune." By "fortune," I'm going to use Earl Nightingale's definition: the goal or achievement you are shooting for.

Access to informative media is one of the biggest advantages we have in today's fast-paced world. Listen to things more than once because every time you do, you learn something new. Repetition will help you discover ways to serve your customer better. In today's competitive world, we must improve daily.

Listen to books on mindset and positive thinking. In life and sales, it is way too easy to focus on the negative. You want to do everything you can to focus on the positive, and, as I've heard Bob Proctor say, "Think of ways that you can do something; don't think of ways that you can't!" Train your brain to develop the habit of looking for the positives in any situation.

I know that is easier said than done, but it is a worthy ideal to work toward. Remember that customers want to do business with people they know, like, and trust—and who are positive. No one wants to do business with a negative person.

Having an Attitude of Gratitude

It is also a good habit to write down five things you are grateful for every day. They don't have to be big things. Having running water, a comfortable home to sleep in, and loving family and friends definitely count. Those are the kinds of things to be very thankful for. It's a good way to live life, and people want to do business with grateful people.

Remember that sales skills can be learned by anyone, not just the "natural born salespeople."

Going Beyond Financial Metrics

There are indicators of success that go beyond the financial. A purposeful leader can define success *beyond* financial metrics and the usual key performance indicators (KPIs) by incorporating other meaningful and relevant measures of success that align with the organization's purpose and values. Here are some ways a purposeful leader can define success:

Customer satisfaction: Customer satisfaction and loyalty indicate how well the organization is delivering on its promises and meeting customer needs.

Employee engagement: This is a key factor in organizational success. A purposeful leader can measure employee engagement via surveys, focus groups, and other methods.

Social impact: We can define success by gauging the organization's social impact. This can include its contributions to the community, environmental sustainability, and social responsibility.

Innovation: To stay competitive and relevant, an entity must innovate. A purposeful leader can measure success here by tracking the organization's innovation metrics, such as the number of new products or services developed or the speed of product development.

Organizational culture: Organizational culture plays a significant role in achieving organizational success. A purposeful leader can measure success by tracking employee retention rates, team performance, and other cultural metrics that reflect the organization's values and purpose.

Talent retention: Purposeful leaders are more likely to retain top talent, which can be measured through retention rates and employee feedback.

Reputation and brand: Purposeful leadership can enhance an organization's reputation and brand, which can be measured through surveys and other methods.

Overall, a purposeful leader can define success by incorporating measures that align with the organization's purpose and values beyond financial metrics and traditional KPIs. By doing so, they can ensure that the organization is achieving its goals and making a meaningful impact on its stakeholders.

> Measure success not only by financial metrics but also by the positive impact you make on individuals, communities, and the world at large.

Impact isn't always able to be measured with traditional metrics, and it can be achieved in many ways. It comes not just through the products, services, or social programs you offer, but also through the stories told by and about your organization.

The Power of Storytelling by Phyllis Jenkins

Are you a leader who wants to connect with your team more effectively and meaningfully? You should incorporate telling stories to help convey a memorable message while building trust.

Storytelling is an ancient art form that dates to the dawn of human civilization and is still a powerful tool for communication in modern society. The power of storytelling in leadership is immense.

When used strategically, storytelling creates an emotional connection between your leadership and members of your organization, encouraging teamwork, creativity, and motivation.

You can use storytelling to share your vision. Whether leading a small business, a large corporation, or any group, you need an inspiring vision of what could be and how to get there. Storytelling allows you to share this vision in a compelling way that resonates with people. You can do this through tales of how others have achieved success or by sharing your own successes and failures.

Identifying the Key Message

Simply telling a story is not enough. To make an impact, leaders should identify the key message they want to convey before sharing their stories. The key message is the central idea or lesson the leader wants their team to take away from the story. This could be a lesson they learned, a mistake they made, a challenge they overcame, or a value they hold dear.

The core idea should be relevant to the team and the organization's goals. For example, if the main point is the importance of persistence, the leader should explain how this value holds significance to the team's current goals or challenges.

Identifying the key message is crucial for several reasons. First, it helps the leader focus their story on a specific point, which can make it more memorable and impactful. A clear message can also help the team relate the story to their own experiences, increasing its relevance and resonance. The story can become cohesive and connected with a well-defined statement, and the team may understand the intended point.

Second, identifying the key message can help the leader prepare for the storytelling. A clear message can guide the leader's choice of words, tone, and delivery. It can help them build a narrative arc that leads to the message and concludes with a call to action or a takeaway. This can make the story more engaging and persuasive.

Third, identifying the key message can help the leader evaluate the effectiveness of their storytelling. If the team doesn't seem to grasp the message or doesn't respond as the leader intended, the leader can review their storytelling and evaluate where they might have missed the mark.

Was the message effectively conveyed or unclear? Perhaps the message the story conveys is not relevant. Sometimes a shorter version is better, and practice can help.

Being Authentic and Vulnerable

As a leader, it is easy to fall into the trap of projecting an image of perfection and infallibility. However, in reality, nobody is perfect. Everyone has their own set of strengths and weaknesses. Being authentic and vulnerable with your team members can help you connect with them on a deeper level, build trust, and foster a culture of openness and honesty. Sharing personal stories, including struggles, failures, and fears, can make you more relatable as a leader.

When you show you are unafraid to admit your mistakes and own up to your failures, your team members will feel more comfortable doing the same. This can create camaraderie and a shared sense of purpose within the team.

When leaders share their struggles and failures alongside their successes and achievements, they become more human and multidimensional to their team members. This can help build mutual understanding, respect, and a positive working relationship. Being open about your own experiences can inspire team members to share their own stories of success and struggle, which can further build trust and openness within the team.

Early in my career, I had a team lead who shared a deeply personal story of caring for his mother, who was battling dementia. Despite the geographical distance that separated them, with his mother residing in another state, he remained steadfast in his commitment to her well-being. With genuine transparency, alongside the regular business information in his weekly newsletter, he shared heartfelt updates about his mother's condition. His vulnerability touched our hearts and fostered a deep sense of understanding and compassion within our group.

Team members walking in similar shoes found the courage to share their stories of hardship and resilience.

This is an excellent example of how being authentic and vulnerable as a leader can also positively impact communication and collaboration. When team members feel understood and heard, they are more likely to share their ideas and perspectives, leading to better teamwork and decision-making. Being open to feedback and willing to admit mistakes can create an environment where team members feel heard and valued and are more inclined to work together toward shared goals. So be brave, be yourself, and watch your team thrive.

Using Vivid and Descriptive Language

Leaders should use vivid and descriptive language to truly engage team members. Aim to paint a picture in listeners' minds using sensory details, emotions, and even dialogue. For example, instead of saying, "I worked really hard to overcome a challenge," a leader could say, "I woke up before dawn every day for weeks, poring over research and analysis, driven by a relentless desire to succeed." This description is more vivid and engaging and helps team members understand the extent of the effort required to overcome the challenge.

Leaders should also incorporate sensory details into their tellings. For example, they could describe the sights, sounds, smells, tastes, or textures of a particular experience. Doing so helps team members visualize the situation more clearly and engage more fully with the story.

An effective technique is to use dialogue in personal stories. Leaders can use direct quotations to bring a story to life and convey emotions more effectively. For example, a leader could say, "I'll never forget what my mentor said to me when I felt discouraged. She told me, 'You have what it takes to succeed. You just need to keep going.'" This quotation helps team members understand the mentor's supportive and encouraging nature and provides actionable advice for team members to follow. Using vivid and descriptive language will help team members relate to the story and remember the key message.

Connect the story to the organization's goals. One mistake many leaders make is focusing on telling personal stories that are disconnected from the organization's goals and vision. While personal stories are essential, as they humanize leaders and make them relatable, connecting these stories to the organization's goals is critical. Leaders should demonstrate how their personal experiences align with the company's mission and vision. That helps team members understand the importance of their work and aids in aligning the team to a common goal.

When leaders use personal stories to connect with their team members and share how their experiences relate to the organization's goals, it has a cascading effect throughout the group, bolstering collaboration and unity. It creates a culture that values learning and growth and a sense of belonging to something larger than oneself. As a result, team members feel more connected, engaged, and happy in their jobs, ultimately leading to greater productivity and success for the organization.

Encouraging Team Members to Share

When building solid teams, leaders need to go beyond just connecting with their members through their own stories. Encouraging team members to share their stories is equally important. Such an environment not only enriches the team's fabric but also allows individuals to be seen and heard. Every team comprises individuals with diverse backgrounds, each member with a unique journey.

When leaders encourage team members to share their stories, they create a tapestry of perspectives that positively influences the entire organization. These narratives, woven together, form the foundation of a vibrant and inclusive workplace where everyone's unique contributions are celebrated.

How can leaders cultivate an environment that nurtures the art of storytelling? There are several approaches to inspire team members to share their stories authentically and fearlessly. One way is organizing storytelling workshops or team-building activities that center around exchanging personal experiences. These interactive sessions create a safe and supportive space for team members to step outside their comfort zones and share their narratives, fostering stronger bonds and mutual respect.

When they share their stories, it can also help leaders identify areas where they need to provide support. For example, if a team member shares about struggling with mental health, leaders can put measures in place to support the team member through their struggles. Encouraging team members to share their stories is an essential element in building a cohesive and supportive team. When leaders create a safe and inclusive environment for team members to share their experiences and perspectives, they can foster deeper connections, build trust, and create a more supportive work environment.

In the Exercises section at the end of this chapter, you'll find questions leaders can use as a guide for sharing personal stories.

Finally, allow me to share my personal story of becoming a leader in helping others, including entrepreneurs and leaders from all walks of life, tell their stories.

In 2010, I founded the Powerful Journey Organization with a simple goal: to provide a platform for women to tell their stories. But what began as a small endeavor has become an impactful movement, setting many people free as they began to take their stories to the stage.

Through Powerful Journey, I have seen the power of storytelling firsthand; we have helped women and men unearth and articulate their unique stories and receive a sense of freedom and liberation. I've seen the light in their eyes when they finally put that last period on their manuscript, the relief mixed with excitement when they hold their published book in their hands, and the joy of impacting others with their words.

Those who listen—hearing stories of pain, struggle, and perseverance—gain a newfound understanding of themselves. Hearing stories of resilience gives people the assurance that they are not alone and that hope still exists for them in whatever situation they find themselves.

The truth is, our stories should never be taken to the grave. Everyone has a story that can resonate with someone else, providing support, solace, and hope. With this knowledge, I urge everyone to find the courage to share their stories—whatever they may be—and allow others to be enriched and comforted by them.

Together, we can create a ripple effect of empowered storytelling and, ultimately, transform the world—one story at a time.

Chapter Recap

Measuring the true impact of purposeful leadership can be challenging, as it goes beyond traditional metrics such as revenue or profit. Ultimately, the impact of purposeful leadership may be difficult to quantify, but its effects can be felt in various aspects of an organization, from employee morale to customer loyalty. Many things contribute to the impact you get to have, including the stories you and others tell.

Exercises

- Make a list of personal stories that have had a significant impact on you.
- Determine how a story aligns with the organization's values and goals.
- Add sensory details and emotions to one story and see how it changes the feeling and impact of it.
- Consider how to use dialogue to make a story more engaging and relatable to your team members.
- Ask yourself the following questions:
  - What is the key message or lesson you want your team members to take away from your personal story?
  - How can you encourage your team members to share their own stories that align with the organization's mission and vision?
  - Which platforms or forums can share personal stories within the organization (e.g., team meetings, company blogs)?
  - How can you ensure personal stories are shared in a respectful and empathetic manner, considering the diversity of experiences and backgrounds among team members?
  - How can personal story sharing be used to build and strengthen relationships among team members?
  - How can the organization encourage a culture of personal story-sharing that fosters openness, creativity, and innovation?

Call to Action

Decide to track your progress and that of your team and organization as a whole. Determine whether you are achieving your goals and fulfilling your purpose.

Chapter 8 Leading with Purpose in Times of Change

"The greatest danger in times of turbulence is not the turbulence; it is to act with yesterday's logic."
—Peter Drucker, *Management: Tasks, Responsibilities, Practices*

Leading with purpose in times of change is critical for the success of any organization. During times of change, leaders must remain focused on their organization's purpose and values and communicate with their team effectively to ensure that everyone is on the same page.

Case Study: Unwelcome Change by Shylla Webb

"Today, I will practice nonjudgment. Today, I will practice nonjudgment. Today, I will practice nonjudgment. I don't know what kind of news I'm about to hear today, but I will practice nonjudgment. Stay neutral at minimum," I recited to myself.

That had become my normal morning self-talk as I looked at myself in the mirror and styled my hair. The world I had always known was changing rapidly, and at times I felt like I was living in *The Twilight Zone*. I couldn't wrap my head around the information being provided and the leadership decisions made from the very top. It wasn't my job to ask questions of the decision-makers; it was my job to carry out the orders.

I keep thinking, *This new mandated change by the federal and state governments is going to put us all under, once and for all.* We didn't have enough time in a day to perform our typical duties, let alone time to add five pages of paperwork to our load.

I had no idea how we were going to make it, and neither did anyone else in the organization when I shared the information with the team I was leading.

"What?! You mean I have to…"

"How could they?"

"What are they thinking?"

"Have they ever done this job?"

"When are we ever going to get a break?"

"Things were bad enough…"

I kept thinking, *Don't shoot the messenger*. Leader down. They shot the messenger.

I was able to recognize we were all in a stage of grief known as shock. We couldn't believe what was being added to our workload and couldn't see a way to get it done.

I listened. I listened some more.

"What are you going to do about this, how will you fix this problem? I'll quit before they mandate I do more paperwork!"

"I can't do anything about their decision. I am here to support you through this in the most effective and efficient way possible. Much like many of you expressed, I too have concerns about this mandate and what it will do to workloads that already seem to stretch everyone too thin. While I don't have any answers, I am confident we are strong enough to pull together and find the answers. I'm sorry, I wish I had more I could offer you other than simply being here with you through this time of difficulty. For now, we have to wait until we get more information for what the solutions are. First step was me communicating to you this change is going to happen."

We were all in shock. I didn't have any magic words, and suddenly it become so quiet, we could've heard a pin drop. I announced that our scheduled time had come to an end, so everyone was welcome to leave and that I planned on staying until all concerns were heard.

Everyone got up and quietly walked out. Most didn't look at me, and those who did look gave me the sympathetic "It sucks to be you" expression.

I returned to my desk and took a deep breath. I sat in silence for a few minutes before opening my email.

The first email was from a staff member who attended that meeting. It said, "I'm sorry staff were yelling at you like they were, and I can't imagine how you felt inside. On the outside, I was impressed with the ease and grace of your response. Thank you for staying so calm."

I smiled, and my heart felt warm.

I hadn't done anything special. In fact, I wished I had been able to do more for the staff to ease their emotions. I had gone into the meeting with no expectations other than to share what I needed to share and listen to their responses with a humble disposition.

I anticipated a few things:

- People will associate this change as being stressful.
- This news would activate high stress levels because it's about a big change.
- Many would likely respond with annoyance, anger, and/or frustration.
- They would respond with shock and most likely some would project their emotional response onto me.

I knew a few things, as well:

- Their stress stemmed from the difference between the reality of the situation and what they believe it should be.
- The staff's responses weren't about me but about them and their ability to cope with change.
- Their ability to respond as openly and honestly as they did demonstrated they trusted me and we had rapport.
- The best solution would be about "we," not "me."
- Change isn't easy for most people.

One of my former leaders, Shawn Gombos, says, "Resistance is predictable." Her phrase played out in my mind many times over the next few days.

Responding

Any time people are presented with an unwanted change, we can expect them to go through a state of shock and/or overwhelm.

Their stress response system will be activated, causing them to fight the change, try to avoid it, or freeze when presented with the change. Everyone will respond in their own way. As a leader, you can model some helpful ways to process it.

As their leader, I was to be an observer of their responses, not to react to them. Even if they were directing their reactions toward me, it required me to take a neutral position and not take it personally.

"Today, I will practice nonjudgment." Sometimes I wasn't convinced that was possible as a human being. What I did know is that statement was creating a higher level of self-awareness within me about when I was judging others and found myself imposing my own beliefs onto how others should act. If nothing else, it was removing the barriers I was using and allowing me to deeply connect with others.

I put myself in the staff's position and wondered what I would need in that type of situation. I realized we all seem to handle the stress of change best when we feel supported and have people to rely on. We all have a deep desire to be seen, heard, and honored wherever we are.

As a leader, I don't have to agree with their feelings and perspectives in order to demonstrate that I value where they are. I see too many leaders make this error of imposing their own expectations of how someone should respond to challenging situations.

As Stephen Covey said, "Begin with the end in mind."

I asked myself, "As the leader, if I want staff to come out of this better, what is the ideal end I have in mind?" Being with the staff I had the honor of leading inspired me to show up powerfully for them.

Being Present

The next morning, my tasks were completed early so that when staff arrived, I could be present and visible.

As thanks for their time the day before, I sent an email to all the staff acknowledging the pressure they must feel and the challenges that come with change. I also reassured them that I was there to walk alongside them on the journey.

For the staff who seemed to be having the most difficulty, I emailed each of them individually to see if they would like to meet with me to discuss the changes further or if I could support them in any way. In response, they either thanked me for being who I am as their leader or apologized for their behavior in the meeting. It is likely that I would not have heard an apology if I hadn't reached out to them.

Connecting

I walked throughout the building that morning, taking care of errands and connecting with staff members as I saw them. Some brought up the changes; others didn't. I allowed each of them to approach me about the topic as they felt they needed to. I just wanted to be present with them.

So much was unknown. In fact, I didn't have any answers, either. I too was feeling a little anxious about the ambiguity of the new direction we were going. Thinking back to all the other times change was sprung upon me, I recognized that things always fell into place. I trusted it would happen that time, too.

As leaders, we get into these positions because we are seen as individuals with authority and knowledge. We typically have most of the answers at our fingertips.

I don't want to be the type of leader that has all the answers. In fact, I don't believe I have them or that I always know best. The team members know the best solutions, and my job was to extract that wisdom from them. Every time I coordinated activities like that, staff felt empowered, deep meaningful conversations were held, and connections were made.

That brought an idea to mind. The next staff meeting we had, I would seek their solutions on how to manage the stress and pressures we were facing.

I was committed to being transparent with them along the way and sharing weekly updates, including letting them know that no more information had been received. All people feel more secure when things are predictable and consistent, even when the events aren't favorable.

Most professionals fear change because they fear failure more. It was important to recognize, and I wanted to celebrate our failures without seeming cheesy or doing some rah-rah event with pom-poms.

Facilitating

First, I needed to know how they viewed their position at work and what they saw was possible. Camaraderie and connection are fostered when people know they are not alone in how they feel and what they think. My first activity was to get them connected and thinking about the past, present, and future.

I posed these questions:

- Think of a specific time in the last three years that you faced an unexpected and unwanted change. What challenges did you face? What lessons did you learn? What were the gifts of that experience?
- Looking back on that experience, what wisdom did you gain? In life? Work? Self? Others? World?
- When it comes to changes happening with the new mandates, what would you like to be celebrating 12 months from now? With self? With your colleagues?

Everyone had a few minutes to answer the questions on their own. Then they were asked to partner up with someone they chose. One person would ask their partner the questions, and they would listen. At the end of the time, the person listening would close the interview by mentioning what they appreciated the most. Next, the person listening would then become the one interviewed.

Together, we were able to acknowledge where we were and where we wanted to go. In addition, we created a list of resiliency tools that people found effective.

As the saying goes, "History repeats itself," and as an intentional leader, I needed to make sure it was the effective parts of our history that repeated. My experience has taught me that people usually flounder when left to their own devices, especially during times of change.

Serving

By taking the time to gather them and facilitate an exchange of personal experience, I created connection, which forms community. By asking them which solutions worked for them, I demonstrated they know best how to lead themselves and each other. By making a list of their most effective tools, I created a resource for capacity building.

There was chatter among the group on the way out, smiles on their faces, and gratitude expressed. Some people even assured me we'd get through the change just fine.

Embrace change as an opportunity for growth, and lead your team through uncertainty with a clear vision, adaptability, and unwavering resilience.

Navigating Change and Uncertainty

Purposeful leaders focus on what they can control and work to find solutions to the challenges they face even while navigating change and uncertainty. This can involve adapting to new circumstances, seeking out new opportunities, or changing direction altogether.

Stay true to your purpose and values. In times like this, it's especially important.

Empower and support your team. Purposeful leaders understand that their success is closely tied to the success of their team.

Foster a culture of resilience. Change and uncertainty can be difficult, but good leaders understand that resilience is key to overcoming challenges. By fostering a culture of resilience, leaders can help their team members bounce back from setbacks and persevere in the face of adversity.

Seek out opportunities for growth and learning. Change and uncertainty can provide valuable opportunities for growth and learning, so seek them out. Purposeful leaders use them to refine their leadership skills and find new ways to make a positive impact.

Adapting

Adapting your vision and strategy to changing circumstances requires an ability to assess the current situation and adjust your plans accordingly. You must have a flexible mindset and anticipate and respond to changes in the business environment, such as shifts in customer needs, market trends, or technological innovations.

You first need to be aware of the changes happening around you. This means staying informed of industry developments, customer preferences, and market trends. You can gather this information through market research, competitor analysis, and customer feedback.

Once you have a clear understanding of the changes, evaluate your existing vision and strategy and identify areas that need to be adjusted. This may involve revising your business model, product offerings, or marketing strategy. It may also require you to redefine your goals and objectives in light of new circumstances.

Throughout the process, it is important to remain true to your purpose and values. Make changes that are aligned with your overall mission and that reflect your commitment to your customers and stakeholders. It also means communicating your updated plan clearly to your team and stakeholders, so that everyone is on the same page and understands the rationale behind the changes.

Key Strategies for Leading with Purpose in Times of Change

Times of change can be tough for everyone. You may find the following strategies helpful.

Communicating your vision: During change, it's important to clearly communicate your vision and the reason for the change. This will help your team members and other stakeholders understand the pivot and feel more comfortable with it.

Staying focused on your purpose: While it's important to adapt to changing circumstances, it's equally important to stay in alignment with your organization's purpose and values. This will help you make the right decisions.

Being transparent: During times of change, be transparent with your team. Share information about the change as it happens, and be open to feedback.

Empowering your team: Change can be stressful for every person on your team, so empower your team members to take ownership of their work and adapt. Provide them with the resources and support they need to be successful.

Leading by example: Effective purposeful leaders lead by example. Show resilience in the face of challenges and display commitment to your organization's purpose and values, even when things get tough.

By doing these things, you can lead with purpose during times of change and ensure that your organization stays focused on its mission and values.

The Empowered Leadership Approach™ by Lee Brower

"A leader without direction is like a ship without a compass, drifting aimlessly in the sea."
—Ken Blanchard

Are you a leader struggling to navigate through today's fast-paced and uncertain business world?

Imagine being in a lifeboat, surrounded by vast rolling waves in all directions. Although equipped with oars, you have no idea which direction to row. But suddenly, you catch a glimpse of land, and now you know exactly where to go. This newfound clarity gives you motivation and purpose.

Likewise, people who lack a clear sense of purpose are like drifters, allowing the world's currents to take them wherever they may. Navigating the abundance of choices and opportunities available to us can be overwhelming. Having too many options can be as limiting as having none at all. This often results in decision paralysis, where the fear of making the wrong choice prevents people from making any decision at all. Having a clear sense of purpose is essential in navigating life's challenges and making meaningful decisions.

In today's Volatile, Uncertain, Complex, and Ambiguous (V.U.C.A.) world, great leadership has taken a backseat to great management. It's disheartening to see a lack of empowering leaders who inspire us to achieve the impossible, like John F. Kennedy's goal of sending a man to the moon or Nelson Mandela's belief that anything can be accomplished. Instead, too often, we see a focus on effective management rather than visionary leadership. Antoine de Saint-Exupéry's quotation captures the essence of true leadership, to inspire and instill a yearning for something greater, rather than just delegating tasks.

"If you want to build a ship, don't drum up the men to gather the wood, divide the work, and give orders. Instead, teach them to yearn for the vast and endless sea."

The world needs leaders who can inspire us to reach beyond what we think is possible and embrace challenges with enthusiasm and determination.

Regrettably, many leaders in our current era seem to be fixated on pointing out what isn't working, instead of inspiring us to improve upon what is working and asking how we can make it even better. This approach fails to motivate us to strive for greater heights and misses the opportunity to build upon our existing strengths.

You don't have to look too far to see examples of poor leadership at the very highest levels of business and government:

1. **Blockbuster:** The video rental chain Blockbuster was slow to embrace digital distribution and failed to see the potential of streaming services like Netflix. They had no inspiring vision for the future and ultimately went bankrupt.
2. **Kodak:** Kodak was a dominant force in the photography industry but failed to adapt to the rise of digital cameras. They had no inspiring vision for the future and ultimately filed for bankruptcy in 2012. Instead of being in the business of capturing memories and preserving history, they focused solely on selling film and cameras.
3. **Brexit:** The British government's handling of the Brexit process was criticized for a lack of inspiring vision and poor communication. The process was marked by indecision, delays, and uncertainty, leading to economic and political instability.
4. **Venezuela:** The Venezuelan government's socialist policies have been criticized for a lack of inspiring vision and poor leadership, leading to economic collapse, political unrest and a humanitarian crisis.

What the world is calling for—or should I say hungering and thirsting for—is what we call Empowered Leadership. In the Empowered Wealth Leadership Approach, "Empowered Wealth" denotes an all-encompassing idea that transcends mere financial means. It includes various types of assets contributing to a rich and satisfying life, such as personal growth, relationships, experiences, and contributions to society. If the past includes everything prior to this moment, and the future comprises everything that occurs after, then isn't it accurate to describe the now as the point where past and future meet?

Clayton Christensen, a renowned Harvard Professor and business consultant known for developing the "disruptive innovation" theory—one of the most influential business ideas of the early 21st century—asserted that exceptional culture is cultivated where businesses and families consistently make sound decisions and understand how to replicate them.

The Empowered Wealth Leadership Approach involves creating a culture that knows how to make sound decisions and can replicate them consistently. In a world where choices are plentiful, having the ability to confidently make decisions can lead to better relationships and opportunities. Imagine being able to pass on this invaluable skill not only to your professional teammates, but also to your children and grandchildren, equipping them to become better decision-makers in an unpredictable and complex world.

Do you think the challenges of navigating a VUCA world will become easier or more difficult over time? Would you rather leave behind a substantial inheritance or a tried-and-true method for making better choices? The latter can be an invaluable gift to your loved ones, empowering them with the skills to navigate an uncertain future.

Choices can only be made in the present moment, not in the past or future. Most choices require quick decision-making within a few seconds. If someone were to say they've never made a bad decision, you would probably find it hard to believe.

In general, decisions are made with positive intentions, such as wanting to be physically fit or financially stable, or have good relationships. However, the challenge lies in the choices we make. For instance, if you decide to prioritize fitness, and your alarm goes off at 5:30 a.m., you have a choice to hit snooze or not. The choices we make in life make us. Every choice you make is either a deposit or withdrawal from our future.

Central to the Empowered Wealth Leadership Approach are three essential leadership responsibilities that foster improved decision-making in the present moment. After all, isn't the now where all choices are made?

Let's delve deeper into the three core responsibilities of an empowered leader within this approach.

Gratitude

Gratitude is a foundational element with leaders fostering an environment of appreciation and positivity. They encourage team members to recognize and express gratitude for their achievements, cultivating a mindset of abundance and openness to further success.

A leader's fundamental role is to cultivate an atmosphere where gratitude is the starting and ending point of all endeavors. We call this Go B.I.G.™—Begin In Gratitude.

This isn't just a superficial nod to thankfulness. Empowered leadership actively upholds and nurtures a gratitude-oriented mindset, irrespective of the situation. Before addressing any difficulties or setbacks, team members must first identify their successes by asking, "What went well, and how can we repeat and make even better and amplify future outcomes?" Maintaining focus on the positives fosters an environment of gratitude and abundance.

From this place of appreciation, they then constructively question their experiences, asking, "Given another chance, and armed with our current knowledge, how could we improve?" This perspective involves everyone fostering an environment ripe for heightened creativity and innovation.

This approach is not only applicable in a professional setting, but it can also be effectively implemented at home. During our children's upbringing, we had a rule: before they could express a complaint about their day, they were invited to share three positive occurrences. Frequently, after sharing three positive experiences, they would forget about their complaint.

I recall numerous end-of-semester conversations where the emphasis was not on their grades. Instead, we concentrated on the empowering question, "If you had the chance to repeat this, armed with the knowledge you now possess, how could you enhance your performance?"

Professionally and personally, by fostering a Go B.I.G. atmosphere, we eliminate space for blame, shame, or justification. This encourages everyone to function within their most creative realm, concentrating entirely on growth and innovation.

To consistently make good choices in the present moment (the Now), you must optimize your past and embrace your future. Your past is a valuable resource and can serve as an exceptional teacher. The question is, who owns your past?

I have posed this question to numerous entrepreneurs, and they all respond, "I do!" However, when I ask if it's an asset or liability, the answers are mixed.

Some view it as an asset, others as a liability, and some say it's both or that it depends on the situation.

But what is the past? The past refers to a period of time that has already occurred, reaching from a moment ago all the way back to the beginning of time. It exists as a concept in our minds, as a collection of memories, experiences, and historical events that have shaped our present reality.

To fully optimize your past, it's essential to reflect on your experiences and learn from them. This is exactly what we do when we Go B.I.G. We are capturing our experiences and by asking why I am grateful for that experience, we put ourselves in an attitude of gratitude instead of an attitude of scarcity.

Learning from Experience

Is there any experience that you cannot learn from? I have asked this questions hundreds of times, and only once did I have someone respond with a firm, "Yes!"

While on a plane, I sat next to a woman who began to vent about her problems to me. I eventually asked her if there was anything in her life that she couldn't learn from.

She responded with her experience with her first husband, which led to more complaints.

I noticed her beautiful wedding ring and inquired about her current marriage.

She paused, sighed, and admitted it was wonderful. She had learned from her previous marriage to make better choices in relationships.

We shared a laugh as she caught herself mid-sentence.

Our past is a tapestry of experiences ranging from everyday to exciting, sad to happy, and even horrible to joyful. When we capture these experiences, whether positive or negative, they become assets that can teach us valuable lessons that we wouldn't have learned otherwise.

Have you ever reread a self-help book or the Scriptures and found something profound that you missed before? This is because our new experiences bring new contexts to previously read material. By continuously learning from our past experiences and applying new insights to future ones, we can continue to grow and evolve. The lessons we learn from our past experiences are only as valuable as the new experiences that help us see them in a new light. When we embrace this cycle of learning and growth, our lives become richer and more fulfilling.

Zolo

This profound connection between our past experiences and our most important choices might not have happened but for an experience I had almost 30 years ago when I was traveling with my son, Bo, on an adventure to Mongolia shortly after the Iron Curtain had come down. This was a life-changing experience that took place at the Mongolian Stock Exchange—the brainchild of a 28-year-old Mongolian gentleman who went by the nickname of Zolo.

The winds of freedom had reached even far-off Mongolia, and young Zolo had conceived the idea for a stock market where investors could trade shares of ventures, just as the rest of the world does. Zolo took great pride in his creation and told us that he frequently led tours for school children, journalists, and anyone else interested in seeing one of the first harbingers of free enterprise to reach the formerly Communist nation.

He shared with us the long hours he put in, sometimes working well past midnight. He told of students lined up outside the doors to learn about democracy and the free enterprise system. They were starving for knowledge.

Zolo's front teeth were chipped. When we spoke about his motivation to work so hard and his devotion to sharing, the conversation turned to what had happened to his teeth. He explained ruefully that the damage was a result of his honest opinion about the state of the Mongolian economy.

Local government officials had to compete in free elections for their seats, a novel experience after decades of Communist rule. These Communist leaders frequently made television appearances during the campaign, in which they assured the nation that the economy was doing great.

Zolo knew otherwise and shared his opinions about the realities of Mongolia's struggling economy with a journalist. After the interview appeared in a local newspaper, Zolo was arrested and brought down to City Hall for a traditional Communist-style interrogation. That's when he suffered the damage to his teeth.

Zolo bore the memory stoically. The next words he spoke electrified me, and as a result, changed my life. "I realized in a flash," he said, after describing the beating, "that everything I possessed could be taken from me—my house, my car, my money. It could all be gone in a flash. But what I have in here"—he tapped his head— "can never be taken from me."

As I was listening to Zolo, I was elbowing Bo. Was he listening? A typical American teenager, he was focused on football and girls. Education was something he had to do, not something he hungered for. For years, I thought *this* was the message. Bo and I talked about the importance of education and the worth of knowledge. It was the lesson we needed to share at that time.

Then, about three years later, I was reading Zolo's account in my journal. Thank goodness for my journal. (Someone once said that a dull pencil is better than a sharp mind.) I had no memory of what Zolo had said when pointing to his head, saying, "what I have in here can never be taken from me."

What followed was even more profound: "What I have in here is of no value to anyone except me. When I die, it will die with me—unless I give it away. When I give it away, it has a life of its own!" A still voice within told me this was incredibly important.

Zolo's stock exchange existed to capitalize assets, to create value by allowing people to benefit from the experience, wisdom, and hard work of others. Rereading Zolo's words, I realized that he was doing the very same thing with his life experience—the assets or memories in his head. He had recognized—and was teaching me—that the knowledge and experiences we hold in our brains are vitally important assets. But to capitalize that asset-to increase its value, we must give it a life of its own. And to do that, we must first capture the experience in writing or verbally share it with others. If we die without sharing those assets with others, the value of our Experience Assets dies as well.

If we own our past, and our past is our greatest teacher, then who owns our future?

Vision

Vision in this context transcends any specific, tangible goals. The Empowered Leadership Approach involves the crucial responsibility of communicating and protecting an **inspiring vision** that inspires team members to aim for unattainable goals while embracing the journey towards growth and improvement. The process of pursuing the vision is just as inspiring as achieving it, and purposeful leaders must emphasize this to encourage growth.

By rigorously promoting a shared vision, we can align team members, foster collaboration, and instill a sense of direction and purpose. Consistently highlighting the vision in all activities fosters a focus on shared aspirations, which promotes greater unity and collaboration within the organization or family.

No vision of the future

Years ago, I had the opportunity to be a volunteer counselor at the Utah State Prison. After a thorough background check, several interviews, and some minor training, I found myself a couple of times a week sitting in front of young prisoners including at least one that was in for murder. One of the many things I took away from the experience is that most of the prisoners I dealt with, especially the repeat offenders, had no concept of the word *future*.

Imagine living life making choices without any thought or influence of a future. Without a future, there are no consequences. The importance of owning our future cannot be overstated, as it provides a framework for making meaningful choices that can positively impact our lives and the lives of those around us. Sadly, many people, including some of our leaders, live each day without a future—without considering the consequences of their actions.

Driven by vision

I once heard an inspiring story from Jim, a successful entrepreneur who was passionate about hiking at high elevations. Jim was eager to share his recent experience on a Rockies trail in Colorado, where he was trekking through snow and admiring the beauty of his surroundings in solitude.

When he heard another hiker approaching from behind, he picked up his pace, determined not to be overtaken. To his surprise, the hiker who slowly passed him was a man in his seventies. Feeling frustrated, Jim summoned the last of his energy and called out, "What drives you?"

The older man slowed down, paused for a moment, and then replied, "My vision of the future sustains me through any present agony."

When Jim told me this story, I was struck by the profound simplicity and truth of the man's words. It perfectly captures the idea that our vision of the future can sustain us and drive us forward, even in the face of adversity. I had to write it down, as it honestly says it all.

Motivation versus Inspiration

Can people be motivated? Of course. Can people be motivated to cheat? Motivation and inspiration, while both powerful forces that drive human behavior, operate on different principles and invoke various aspects of our psyche.

Motivation is often linked to specific goals or rewards, and it can be driven by external factors such as incentives, fear, or pressure. In this context, individuals might be motivated to cheat if they believe it will help them achieve a desired outcome, such as winning a game, getting a promotion, or passing an exam. The motivation to cheat might also stem from a desire to avoid negative consequences, such as failure or punishment.

Inspiration, on the other hand, is a more positive and uplifting force that moves us to act in alignment with our values, aspirations, and higher sense of purpose. It often stems from intrinsic factors, including personal growth, passion, or a desire to contribute to something larger than oneself.

In general, people are inspired to act in ways that are consistent with their ideals and beliefs, and cheating typically runs counter to these principles.

As such, while people might be motivated to cheat under certain circumstances, it is unlikely they would be inspired to do so. Inspiration tends to encourage actions that reflect our best selves. Cheating, which involves deceit and dishonesty, is not aligned with this.

Our approach prioritizes crafting a compelling vision that resonates deeply with individuals, prompting them to collaborate effectively toward shared objectives. This approach recognizes that the journey itself, marked by significant milestones, brings its own sense of achievement and fulfillment.

When individuals are inspired by a common cause, they are more likely to work harmoniously, enhancing not only productivity but also workplace relationships and morale.

Moreover, as they journey together toward this shared vision, they experience the satisfaction of passing milestones along the way. These milestones serve as markers of progress, offering tangible proof of their collective efforts and providing motivation for continued work.

Challenge

Great leaders continually challenge the status quo. I often say, "Managers challenge what is not working; leaders challenge what is working." That is not to say that leaders should not be good managers. As they build their organization with supportive managers, efficient systems, and proper communication, leaders are free to spend more time innovating. In today's VUCA world, if you are not challenging especially the things that are working, you are not an empowered leader.

In 2007, our son Nick, then 18 years old and in high school, complained of a bruised cheek he sustained from a basketball game. After he had been through days of pain and several unsuccessful doctor and dentist visits, a CT scan revealed a tumor the size of a baseball in Nick's sinus. It was pushing into his eye.

He was diagnosed with Stage Four cancer.

Nick underwent surgeries, chemotherapy, and radiation for a full year.

Two top specialists in the field disagreed on the best course of action following his treatment, one advising removal of half of his mouth, nose, and one eye; and the other recommending against it.

Nick chose to have the tumor debris removed and to reassess it after surgery. In an unexpected turn of events, the surgeon could find no evidence of disease. Joy and hope filled our hearts.

For the subsequent year, Nick relished the typical life of a twenty-year-old, balancing school, work, and play. At his routine quarterly check-up, the doctor's entrance bore an ominous air. We felt instantly something was wrong.

"Nick," the doctor began solemnly, "a tumor has been found. It's not in your sinuses anymore, but in your spleen and on your pancreas. It's spreading swiftly, and we need to admit you to the hospital tomorrow."

We were all dumbfounded and heartbroken, words failing us.

Eventually, Nick broke the silence. He raised his head and said, "No, I won't have the surgery this week." He then turned to me and added, "Schedule that skydiving trip; I'll come in on Monday."

There is a quotation by Johann Wolfgang von Goethe that I hold dear: "Things that matter most must never be at the mercy of things which matter least." In today's fast-paced, information-saturated world, we are often bombarded by issues and tasks that are deemed very important, creating a whirlwind of choices. Determining what truly matters can be a daunting task. Hence, I have reinterpreted Goethe's quote to resonate with our times and to align with The Empowered Leadership Approach: "Don't let the essential be at the mercy of those things that are very important."

Was it very important for Nick to check into the hospital the very next day? Did it align with what was essential to him? Guided by his vision for the future and maintaining an attitude of abundance, Nick discerned his essentials.

On Friday, Nick and I flew to San Diego, where we enjoyed a Padres game and met a highly experienced Navy SEAL named Nix, who had offered to tandem skydive with Nick on Saturday morning. Regrettably, due to rain, we were grounded. That presented us with the opportunity to visit the Navy SEALs headquarters, where Nick deftly navigated the obstacle course designed for Hell Week. His confidence was palpable. He was strong with a full head of hair. The following day was Easter Sunday, and it was beautiful outside.

After we obtained permission from our families to stay longer, Nick performed a double somersault out of the plane, spun around, and at the last minute, they pulled the chute. I will forever remember Nick's face as he confidently walked toward us with a beaming smile, declaring, "Now, I am ready."

Changing Environment

Not letting the things that are very important get in the way of your essential is especially important in today's VUCA world. The speed at which global information is doubling has increased dramatically since 1900. In 1900, the amount of information being generated globally was much smaller, and it took much longer for information to double.

With the rapid pace of technological advancement and the growth of digital technologies and artificial intelligence, the speed at which information is generated and shared has increased significantly. It is estimated that in 1900, the amount of information being generated globally would double in 50 years. By 1960, they were saying every 2 years. And today, they are saying *every 2 days*.

The responsibility to challenge the status quo is essential for fostering better decision-making at all levels. Leaders encourage their teams to question existing practices and assumptions, to seek out innovative solutions, and to continually strive for improvement. This culture of constructive challenge enables individuals and organizations to adapt, innovate, and thrive in an ever-changing environment.

Harness gratitude to meticulously extract lessons from the past, using them to enlighten the present moment. Fuel inspiration and drive actions in the present. If our past is the source of our wisdom, and our future is the beacon of our inspiration, then what truly transpires only in the present moment?

Three crucial elements transpire only in the present moment:

1. **Gratitude:** Gratitude is experienced in the now. While you can appreciate past events or feel grateful for a hopeful future, the sensation of gratitude is genuinely felt in the present moment. Harnessing an attitude of abundance rather than scarcity while reflecting on your experiences allows you to view them creatively and constructively, determining how to enhance future experiences.

2. **Choice:** Most decisions we make are aspirational. Daily, we make numerous decisions, but the actualization of these decisions occurs in the present. For instance, you might decide you want to get in shape, but when the alarm rings at 5:30 am, the choice to get up or hit the snooze button happens in that moment. It is these choices

that shape us and steer our life's direction. A simple yes or no can lead us down opposite paths.

3. **Action:** Movement is rooted in the present moment. Informed by past experiences and inspired by future visions, action is paramount. Without movement, learning cannot take place. Ask yourself, "What is the smallest step I can take today that will bring me closer to my vision?"

I refer to this process as "Stacking Moments." It's a leadership approach that combines insights from past experiences with a compelling future vision.

As you continue to act, you stack these moments. This sequence of stacked moments creates momentum, a crucial element in effective leadership. Isn't that what leadership is truly about?

STACKING MOMENTS™

1. Gratitude
2. Choice
3. Motion

FUTURE VISION

INFORMS

INSPIRES

TEACHER
PAST

NOW
MOMENTUM

Never underestimate the power of your actions and decisions as a purposeful leader. With every choice, you have the potential to shape a better future and leave a lasting legacy.

137

Transparent Communication

During times of change, it is crucial for leaders to communicate transparently and empathetically. Leaders should be honest and clear about what is happening and why, and show empathy for the concerns and feelings of those who are impacted by whatever is taking place.

Effective communication during turbulence can help to reduce uncertainty and anxiety, build trust and credibility, and create a sense of shared purpose and direction. Leaders should listen actively to their team members, address their questions and concerns, and provide regular updates as the situation evolves.

Leaders should also use their emotional intelligence and self-awareness during these times. They should keep their composure while acknowledging and validating the emotions of their team members. This can help create a positive and supportive culture that fosters resilience and adaptability.

Chapter Recap

Even in times of upheaval, purpose serves as a steadfast guide, illuminating the path toward a brighter future. Step forward, knowing that your unwavering commitment to purpose will lead your people through the storms and toward a horizon of endless possibilities.

Exercises

Vision Communication: Take a scenario where change is happening within your organization. Practice communicating your vision and the rationale behind the change to your team. Clearly articulate the purpose of the change and ensure your team understands and feels comfortable with it.

Purpose Focus: Reflect on your organization's purpose and values. Identify a challenging situation where you need to make a decision. Evaluate whether the decision aligns with your organization's mission and values. Practice staying focused on your purpose while adapting to changing circumstances.

Transparency Practice: Choose a recent change that occurred within your organization. Role-play being transparent with your team by sharing information about the change as it unfolds. Encourage open communication and be receptive to feedback from your team.

Leading by Example Exercise: Reflect on past challenges you have faced as a leader. Consider how you demonstrated resilience and commitment to your organization's purpose and values. Identify strategies that helped you stay focused during difficult times. Role-play scenarios where you exhibit resilience and lead by example to inspire your team.

Call to Action

Write out a plan for how you will create a supportive environment for your team during times of change, delegate responsibilities, and provide resources and support to empower them.

Chapter 9: Becoming a Purposeful Leader for Life

"Leadership and learning are indispensable to each other."
—John F. Kennedy,
Undelivered speech for Dallas, Tx, November 22, 1963

Becoming a purposeful leader for life is not just about mastering a set of skills or achieving a certain level of success. It's a continuous journey of growth and self-discovery.

You must cultivate a strong sense of purpose and a growth mindset, which means knowing why you do what you do, embracing challenges, seeking feedback, and learning from everything and everyone you can. Read on a regular basis, take courses or classes, and seek mentorship. Approach each day with curiosity, humility, and a willingness to try new things, take risks, and push yourself.

To sustain your purposeful leadership journey, it's important to practice self-care. That means attending to your physical, mental, and emotional well-being. This includes getting enough sleep, exercise, and healthy food as well as engaging in activities that bring you joy, such as hobbies, travel, or spending time with loved ones.

Becoming a purposeful leader for life means embracing the power of community—building meaningful relationships with others who share your values, vision, and purpose. The 48 Days Eagles community and Platform Launchers both provide support, accountability, and inspiration, and they help you stay connected to the needs of the world around you and to see opportunities for positive impact.

By embracing the right principles, you can become a purposeful leader who makes a positive impact on your team, your organization, and the world around you, for years to come.

Purposeful leadership is not just about individual growth and development or "the bottom line." It is also about having a positive effect on others and society as a whole. Purposeful leaders should seek to inspire and empower others, cultivating purpose and meaning within their teams and organizations. They should also strive to create positive social and environmental impact through their work.

As a purposeful leader, it is important to recognize that refining your purpose and vision may be an ongoing process. The world and your organization will continue to change, and your purpose and vision should evolve with it. Here are some things to keep in mind as you revise your vision.

Strategies

Embrace a growth mindset. A growth mindset allows you to be open to new ideas, perspectives, and experiences. The belief that you can learn and improve is the core of a growth mindset. Stay curious, adaptable, and open to refining your purpose and vision as needed.

Connect to your stakeholders. These people include your employees, customers, partners, and community members. If you run an online business or organization, that community may not reside in your geographic area, but you still have a community. Regularly ask for feedback from your stakeholders, seeking to understand their needs, expectations, and values. This will help ensure that your purpose and vision are relevant and aligned with what they want and need from you.

Reflect on your experiences. Some say experience is the best teacher. It's not. Evaluated experience is the best teacher. By mulling things over, you may gain insights regarding what worked and what didn't. Take time to think about what you have learned. What could you do better? Write out what you want to achieve in the future. This will help you refine your purpose and vision based on your own experiences.

Stay informed. The world is constantly changing, so stay informed about trends, innovations, and best practices in your industry and beyond. If you do this, you will be better equipped to refine your purpose and vision based on the latest insights.

Be open to collaboration: Collaborating with others can help you gain new perspectives and insights that can inform your purpose and vision. Seek out opportunities to collaborate with others, both within and outside of your organization, to expand your thinking and refine your purpose and vision.

Continuously refine your purpose and vision: You can stay true to your values and goals while also adapting to changing circumstances and opportunities.

Purposeful leadership is not just about achieving success during your tenure as a leader. It is also leaving a lasting legacy that inspires and influences future generations. By intentionally aligning your personal and organizational purpose, creating a positive culture, empowering and developing your team, and leading with empathy and resilience, you can create a meaningful impact that extends beyond your time in leadership.

To leave a lasting legacy through purposeful leadership, consider the following:

Define your legacy. Start by reflecting on the impact you want to have and what you want to be remembered for as a leader. Articulate your legacy in clear, concise language that is easily understood and communicated.

Lead by example. Your actions as a leader speak louder than words. Model the behaviors and values that you want your team to embody and inspire them to do the same.

Invest in your team. Empower your team to grow and develop, both personally and professionally. Encourage them to pursue their passions and interests, and provide opportunities for them to learn and expand their skills.

Give to the community. As a purposeful leader, you have the power to make a positive impact beyond your organization. Find ways to serve your community through volunteer work or philanthropy.

Be open to feedback. Continuously seek feedback from your team, stakeholders, and mentors to ensure that you are staying true to your purpose and values, and making a meaningful impact. Use this feedback to make adjustments and improvements to your leadership approach.

Continuously learn and grow. Purposeful leadership is a lifelong journey. Stay curious and open-minded, and seek out opportunities to learn and grow as a leader.

By embracing purposeful leadership as a lifelong journey, you can create a lasting legacy that inspires and influences future generations of leaders.

Another Note from Dan Miller

Purposeful leadership is not a destination; it's a lifelong journey of self-reflecting, learning, and adapting. Doing it well requires being open to feedback and embracing change along the way.

This is not just about personal success or financial gain. Purposeful leadership is about making a positive impact on society and the world. It's about creating a culture of trust, transparency, and empathy, where team members are empowered to reach their full potential.

Here's the beautiful thing: purposeful leadership is not exclusive to those in formal leadership positions. Each and every one of us has the ability to lead with purpose in our personal and professional lives. It could be as simple as setting a positive example, mentoring others, or treating others with kindness and respect.

To embark on this journey, it's crucial to align your passions, talents, and values with a sense of purpose. Discover what truly drives you, what brings you joy, and how you can use your unique God-given strengths to serve others. This self-discovery lays the foundation for your leadership journey.

It doesn't stop there. Developing emotional intelligence is key. It's about cultivating self-awareness, empathy, and effective communication skills. Understanding your own emotions and triggers as well as tuning into the needs and perspectives of others will allow you to lead with intention and authenticity.

And let's not forget the importance of vulnerability and lifelong learning. Purposeful leaders embrace both. They remain open to new experiences and invest in themselves, seeking out mentors and like-minded individuals who can support and challenge them. This includes joining communities and masterminds that fit their goals. The 48 Days Eagles Community is a low-cost starting point for purposeful leaders.

In conclusion, my friends, purposeful leadership is an ongoing journey that requires continuous self-reflection, growth, and adaptation. It's about aligning your passions, talents, and values with a sense of purpose, leading with intention, authenticity, and a commitment to serving others. So, let's commit to being purposeful leaders who make a difference, not only in our own lives but also in the lives of those around us. Here's to the incredible journey ahead!

Exercises

- **Reflection:** Consider whether you are communicating your purpose, vision, and strategies to your team effectively. Are they engaged and motivated to achieve our goals? Ask yourself, "What is my personal purpose, and how does it align with the purpose of my organization?"
- **Trust-Building Activity:** Organize a team-building exercise or workshop focused on building trust and rapport within your team. Encourage open and honest communication, active listening, and team collaboration for a positive work environment. Reflect on it and discuss ways to apply the principles in day-to-day interactions.
- **Feedback and Coaching Practice:** Select a team member and schedule a feedback and coaching session. Provide constructive feedback on their performance, strengths, and areas for improvement. Collaborate with them to set specific goals and create an actionable development plan. Follow up periodically to provide guidance and support their growth. Reflect on your feedback and coaching style, seeking opportunities to refine and enhance your approach.
- **Innovation and Continuous Improvement Initiative:** Initiate an innovation challenge or improvement project within your team or organization. Encourage team members to share ideas, collaborate, and experiment with new approaches. Provide a platform for brainstorming and prototype testing. Celebrate successes and discuss lessons learned. Evaluate the impact of the initiative on team performance and consider ways to sustain an innovative and continuously improving culture.
- **Balanced Success Measurement Exercise:** Reflect on your organization's current success metrics. Identify additional non-financial metrics or key performance indicators (KPIs) that can measure the team's impact on team members, customers, and society. Discuss

with your team the importance of these metrics and collaborate to define meaningful goals aligned with broader positive impacts.

- **Change Navigation Simulation:** Create a simulated scenario of a change or uncertain situation. Evaluate your vision and strategy in light of these changing circumstances. Adapt your vision, communicate changes effectively to your team, and adjust the strategy accordingly. Reflect on the experience and capture lessons learned to refine your approach to purposeful leadership during times of change.
- **Purpose and Vision Reflection Exercise:** Regularly set aside time for reflection and refinement of your purpose and vision. Engage in self-reflection, journaling, or discussions with mentors or trusted colleagues. Continuously refine your purpose and vision to ensure they align with your personal values and the evolving needs of your team and organization. Consider how your purposeful leadership can leave a lasting legacy.

Chapter Recap

Being a purposeful leader for life is not a destination but a journey and a lifelong commitment. Embracing purpose as a guiding force, we embark on a continuous quest to grow, evolve, and make a lasting impact, knowing that our purposeful leadership will leave a profound legacy for generations to come.

Call to Action

Join a group of purposeful leaders. Here are two that are excellent (some of the coauthors of this book are members of one or both of them). Surround yourself with people you want to be like.

- Platform Launchers https://www.platformlaunchers. com/a/2147508408/RtHkHADV
- 48 Days Eagles Community https://www.48dayseagles. com/a/10052/Z27q6rCH

References

Berger, W. The secret phrase top innovators use. *Harvard Business Review*. (2012, Sept. 17). https://hbr.org/2012/09/the-secret-phrase-top-innovato

Bryson, J.M. *Strategic planning for public and nonprofit organizations: A guide to strengthening and sustaining organizational achievement* (5th ed.). Wiley, 2018.

Goleman, D. *Emotional Intelligence: Why it can matter more than IQ*. New York: Bloomsbury, 1996.

Görgens-Ekermans, G., and Roux, C. "Revisiting the emotional intelligence and transformational leadership debate: n(How) does emotional intelligence matter to effective leadership?." *SA Journal of Human Resource Management* 19 (2021): 1279.

Lubbadeh, T. "Emotional intelligence and leadership–the dark and bright sides." *Modern Management Review XXV,* (2020): *27*, 39—50.

Reina, C. S., Rogers, K. M., Peterson, S. J., Byron, K., & Hom, P. W. "Quitting the boss? The role of manager influence tactics and employee emotional engagement in voluntary turnover." *Journal of leadership & organizational studies*, *25*(1), (2018): 5—18.

Salovey, P., Mayer, J. D., Caruso, D., & Lopes, P. N. "Measuring emotional intelligence as a set of abilities with the Mayer-Salovey-Caruso Emotional Intelligence Test." In S. J. Lopez & C. R. Snyder (Eds.), *Positive psychological assessment: A handbook of models and measures*. American Psychological Association. (2003): 251—265.

DAN MILLER

Dan Miller is author of the *New York Times* best-selling **48 Days to The Work You Love**, *Wisdom Meets Passion, No More Dreaded Mondays,* and *An Understanding Heart*. His 48 Days Podcast consistently ranks in the top 1% of all podcasts worldwide, and his 48DaysEagles.com community is viewed as an example around the world for those seeking to find—or create—the work and life they love.

Dan has been married to his best friend Joanne for over 55 years. They have three grown children and seventeen grandchildren and live in their version of paradise in Osprey, Florida.

He often says, "The best way to predict your future is to create it" and "Stay inspired."

Connect with Dan:

www.48Days.com

www.48DaysEagles.com

PHYLLIS JENKINS

Phyllis Jenkins is s an author, book coach, blogger, international speaker, podcast host, and Powerful Journey founder.

Her ultimate goal is empowering women to take their stories to the stage, not the grave. She also helps them turn their visions into realities by writing books and building a profitable brand.

Phyllis awards two annual education scholarships: The Madian Chumbley scholarship, awarded to a single mom of a special needs child, and the Mildred Ida Byrd Pugh Scholarship to a graduating high school senior. Phyllis' mantra is Live Powerful! Give Powerful!

She is the author of seven books, including volumes I and II of the Telling Our Stories Anthology. Phyllis looks forward to launching her newest book, *You Must Tell Your Story*.

She is celebrating 45 years of marriage to her college sweetheart, Dave. They have two adult daughters and three amazing grandchildren who call her Nana J.

Grab a Free copy of the "My Significant Story Blueprint" at https://phyllisjenkins.com

Connect with Phyllis:

https://www.youtube.com/phyllisjenkins

https://www.linkedin.com/in/phyllis-jenkins-660ba23a

https://www.instagram.com/phyllis_jenkins

https://www.facebook.com/PhyllisByrdJenkins

JOHN BUCHY

John Buchy (pronounced Beeky) is the host of the *Teach Yourself Sales* podcast. He spent 30-plus years in sales, primarily in food-service distribution—an industry with very low margins. John started a podcast to talk about the things that he has learned to pass on his unique experience in the sales world. It is geared primarily toward distribution sales but is relevant to all industries and facets of sales. He wants to teach people how to build relationships with their customers to build their sales.

John has been an aspiring author and is very excited about the opportunity to contribute to the "Purposeful Leadership Anthology"

John also wants to inspire people to not be intimidated by the word *sales*. He offers instead to think of sales as serving not being salesy!

Connect with John:

https://www.facebook.com/john.buchy

COLEEN LAW, PHD

Colleen is a follower of Jesus. She holds degrees in public health and in mental health policy, is an assistant professor at Liberty University, where she teaches public health courses. She is a certified coach and DiSC specialist with the Dan Miller team and serves as a trainer in financial stewardship at Bethel World Outreach Church in Brentwood, TN.

In 2020, Colleen founded ABD Coaching Solutions, a business designed to assist doctoral candidates complete their dissertations in one year. In 2023, ABD Coaching expanded to include life coaching.

Today, Colleen is working on a book to accompany the wok she does with doctoral students. She is also the developer of a course titled Do You Think You Are Worthy?

As a special offer to readers of this anthology, ABD Coaching Services is offering $1,000 in free life coaching to the first 10 people who sign up for discovery calls on the website.

Connect with Colleen:

colleen.e.law@icloud.com

www.linkedin.com/in/colleenelaw

www.facebook.com/colleenlaw

colleenlaw@abdcoachingsolutions.com

AMY HAMILTON, PMP

Amy S. Hamilton is a project manager, author, motivational speaker, and shoe aficionado. She is an award-winning public speaker and has presented in over twenty countries on overcoming adversity, reaching your dreams, computer security, and project management. She has worked at both the US European Command and the US Northern Command & North American Aerospace Defense Command (NORAD) on multiple communications and IT projects.

Amy holds a Bachelor of Science (BS) in Geography from Eastern Michigan University, a Master of Science (MS) in Urban Studies from Georgia State University, Master in Computer Science (MSc) from the University of Liverpool, Master Certificate in Project Management (PM) and Chief Information Officer (CIO) from the National Defense University, and completed the US Air University, Air War College. She has a Doctorate of Philosophy (PhD) in Organizational Leadership. She currently works for the United States Department of Energy as a Senior Cybersecurity Advisor and is detailed to the National Defense University College of Information and Cyberspace.

Connect with Amy:

www.amyshamilton.com

https://www.facebook.com/amyshamiltonpmp

https://www.instagram.com/amyshamiltonpmp

https://www.linkedin.com/company/amyshamilton-com

REVEREND CHARITY GOODWIN

As a mom, pastor, podcaster, author, and one who has suffered panic attacks and body breakdowns from stress and anxiety, Rev. Charity Goodwin's continual journey is to support others to honor and navigate feelings and their place in life, leadership, and spirituality.

Rev. Goodwin is a speaker on leadership as well as spiritual wholeness and emotional wellness. She's the Pastor of Spiritual Formation & Groups at The Gathering in St. Louis, Missouri. She strengthens her ministry with certifications in Emotional Intelligence from Six Seconds as well as the research of Dr. Brené Brown.

She's the author of *GET UP: Unearthing your Passion and Taking Brave Action in 50 Days*. In her podcast *Where Faith & Feelings Meet*, she shares wisdom and practical tools at the intersection of faith and emotions. She's Mom to Gabriel and Levi.

To access the blog and podcast, visit www.charitygoodwin.com

For the free Prevent Burnout Kit: https://mailchi.mp/ffa846d3d962/wbrfec3v9a

Connect with Charity:

https://www.charitygoodwin.com/blog

RENEE METTY, MA

Having over twenty years of experience working with individuals, teams, and organizations in high-pressure situations, Renee Metty is skillful at facilitating change with ease, navigating uncertainty, and making the seemingly impossible possible.

Her unique blend of experience from corporate, leadership coaching and development, education, and entrepreneurship allows Renee to understand the inner workings of human capacity.

Renee has helped everyone from the home to the C-Suite and loves working with professionals to help them perform at their best.

Years of mindfulness practice and her continual journey of deeper self-understanding have prepared Renee to guide others in accessing their own skills, capacities and insights, ultimately allowing them to close the gap from where they currently are to where they want to go. Renee's approach and methodology are influenced by her mentor, a former Olympian and elite performance coach who works with some of the biggest brands and champions in the world. She is studying to be an Equine Gestaltist partnering with horses to heal the hearts of humans and remove deeply rooted beliefs that get in the way. Renee is a wife, a mom of three teenagers, and a PhD candidate working on her dissertation focused on how leaders develop capacity.

Connect with Renee:

www.linkedin.com/in/reneemtty

www.instagram.com/withpause

www.facebook.com/withpause

RON PRICE, MA

Author, speaker, and humorist Ron Price holds a BA in Sociology from the University of Rhode Island and an MA in Counseling from the University of New Mexico. By God's Grace, he has written three books: *PLAY NICE in Your Sandbox at Work* (2016), *PLAY NICE in Your Sandbox at Home* (2018), and *PLAY NICE in Your Sandbox at Church* (2020).

Ron has also created two online video courses: CPR Mastery, in which *CPR* stands for Conflict Prevention and Resolution, is for businesses and secular organizations; PLAY NICE in God's Sandbox is for churches and faith-based small groups.

In 1980, Ron married Maridell, a registered nurse for 36 years. Though they have no children, they have had a few dogs over the years and way too many cats. Ron has also been a Big Brother to six boys through his local Big Brothers/Big Sisters agency.

Since 1997, Ron has owned and operated Productive Outcomes, Inc., which is primarily a speaking, training, and dispute-resolution practice. He has completed over 700 hours of continuing education, mostly in the fields of facilitation, mediation, and relationship skills-building.

In his spare time, he enjoys pickleball, disc golf, and hiking the Grand Canyon.

Connect with Ron:

https://www.facebook.com/ron.price.5891

https://ronprice.com

PHIL MERSHON

Phil Mershon is director of experience for Social Media Examiner, where for over 12 years, he has created amazing customer experiences at events like Social Media Marketing World. He is author of the book *Unforgettable: the Art and Science of Creating Memorable Experiences* and offers speaking and consulting services. Throughout his career of 30+ years, Phil has been creating memorable experiences for businesses like Koch Industries, non-profits, schools, and churches.

Phil is also a jazz saxophonist, pickleball enthusiast, and songwriter. Phil lives in Wichita, Kansas, with his wife Audrey, their three adult children, and their standard poodle, Millie the Therapy Dog.

Connect with Phil:

www.philmershon.com

https://instagram.com/Phil_Mershon

https://twitter.com/Phil_Mershon

https://www.linkedin.com/in/philmershon

https://www.facebook.com/phil.mershon

MYHRIAH YOUNG

Myhriah Young lives in Saratoga Springs, Utah, with her amazing husband, Alex, dog Snuffaluffagus "The Fluffy" Young, and her in-laws. Myhriah and Alex are empty nesters building a life of adventure and impact.

Myhriah loves helping people to live life creatively and feels very fortunate to get to work with the 48 Days team, collaborate with the 100 Cups team, and help other clients in reaching their sales and leadership goals.

She is the hostess of the LinkedIn Live Show: Delightful DiSCussions.

Connect with Myhriah:

https://www.linkedin.com/in/myhriah-young

https://www.facebook.com/myhriahyoung

TAD DICKEL, PHD

Dr. Tad Dickel is the President of T.A. Dickel Group, LLC, in Evansville, Indiana. He is a strategy, leadership, and creativity consultant who specializes in strategic planning, leadership development, and creative problem solving. His clients include businesses, universities, nonprofits, government entities, churches, and schools.

With a career beginning in education, Tad has served as a non-public high school president, principal, and teacher. He regularly teaches graduate courses at Creighton University and University of Evansville in leadership and strategic planning.

Tad holds a PhD in Educational Leadership from Indiana State University, a Certificate in Family Business Advising from FFI-GEN, a Foundations of Design Thinking Certificate from IDEO U, a Certificate in Nonprofit Board Consulting from BoardSource, a Certificate in Fundraising Management from The Fund Raising School. He is a Certified Basadur Simplexity Facilitator and Trainer and a Certified Myers-Briggs Type Indicator (MBTI®) Practitioner. In 2019, Tad was named to the Evansville (Indiana) *Courier & Press*'s "20 Under 40" cohort for his professional accomplishments and service to the community.

Connect with Tad:

tadickel.com

facebook.com/tadickel

linkedin.com/company/tadickel

tad@tadickel.com

JAMES WOOSLEY

James Woosley is an underachiever—only because he's constantly expanding his potential by doing something amazing, then immediately striving for more, knowing that his mind, body, and spirit have been stretched to a new level of possibility.

A former US Air Force officer, and certified project management professional, James is the author of *Conquer the Entrepreneur's Kryptonite: Simple Strategic Planning for You and Your Business* and *Challenge Accepted!: A Simple Strategy for Living Life on Purpose.*

As a book designer and publisher, James has worked on more than 200 books, including *New York Times* bestselling author Dan Miller's self-described magnum opus, *An Understanding Heart.*

Beyond serving his clients, James is a founding member of the Satsuma City School System and former president of the Alabama Association of School Boards. James is a dedicated husband to his high school sweetheart, Heather, father to Anna and Ian, and grandfather of the most beautiful baby girl in the world, Finley.

Connect with James:

https://www.FreeAgentPress.com

https://www. FreeAgentPress.com/mastermind

james@freeagentpress.com

JOANNA HIOE

Joanna Hioe is from Singapore and is currently a PhD student at the National University of Singapore researching natural disasters in Southeast Asia. Alongside that, she is an active contributor in the circles she is in, including her campus, church and other creative communities. As a student of growth and leadership, she is a member of the Maxwell Leadership Team.

She is the author of two books (forthcoming): *Namechanger* and *Shifting Seasons*, which speak of how God changes our stories and how we can respond well to crises. She hopes that her writing can help people feel seen and inch them closer toward living their best and most original lives as God intended.

Connect with Joanna:

https://www.linkedin.com/in/joannahioe

https://twitter.com/@drjoonthego

LEE BROWER

Lee Brower is the founder and chief empowerment officer of Empowered Wealth, LLC, an international "business-family" consulting, coaching, and mentoring firm, and The Business Family Coach™ creator. Using a proprietary coaching model, he applies the Empowered Wealth System™ in both businesses and families. He is also the founder of Th'Rivers™, a community of Arrows Out™ driven entrepreneurs who are inspired by providing selfless leadership.

Author of *The Brower Quadrant*, Lee has made numerous media appearances and keynote addresses around the world. As an international advocate for gratitude, Lee has been featured in the best-selling book and movie *The Secret* and has appeared on numerous television, podcasts, and radio shows, including *The Today Show*.

His breakthrough concepts on preserving true wealth from one generation to the next are changing the landscape of leadership in families, businesses, and communities. Lee is truly a "change agent" of our time. He is dedicated to revolutionizing how entrepreneurially minded leaders can use their influence to create stability at home, at work, and beyond. In short, Lee builds bridges that connect the very best individuals, families, and businesses to their brightest and biggest future.

Connect with Lee:

www.empoweredwealth.com

https://www.facebook.com/EmpoweredWealth

https://twitter.com/EmpoweredWealth

https://www.linkedin.com/in/lee-brower-0365374

AMANDA KELLY

Amanda Kelly is a visionary entrepreneur who thrives on turning the seemingly impossible into a reality. In 2014, she founded A New Dae, a dynamic operational efficiency consulting agency, driven by her unwavering belief that every challenge holds a solution waiting to be discovered. With an unparalleled passion for continuous improvement, Amanda embraces each new day as an opportunity to create positive change. Through her exceptional intentionality and thoughtful dedication, she has proven that nearly anything is achievable.

Amanda's academic journey led her to acquire a Bachelor of Science degree from The University of Tulsa and Texas A&M University Texarkana. Initially delving into the realm of law, she honed her skills and knowledge as an investigative paralegal. It wasn't long before Amanda's entrepreneurial spirit beckoned her to pursue her dreams full-time with A New Dae.

Over the past decade, Amanda has become an invaluable asset to entrepreneurs and CEOs from diverse backgrounds. Her profound impact lies in equipping them with the essential tools to reclaim their time and immerse themselves in the aspects of their businesses they excel at and enjoy doing. Her extensive client portfolio has afforded her unique insights into the common obstacles hindering business owners from reaching their full potential. Drawing from this wealth of experience, Amanda has crafted an innovative organizational methodology that can help any person understand how to get started and successfully achieve their desired results.

Beyond her professional endeavors, Amanda derives immeasurable joy from enhancing the lives of others. She wholeheartedly embraces her calling as a catalyst for positive change, dedicating her time and resources to animal rescue efforts. She was born in Texarkana, Texas and has been living in Houston with her daughter, Presley, for the past decade. Amanda shares her home with a menagerie of animals, adding a touch of liveliness to her family's daily lives. In her free time, she enjoys traveling and going on adventures with her family.To discover more about Amanda Kelly's transformative work or to engage in thought-provoking discussions, please visit her website at www.anewdae.com.

Connect with Amanda:

https://anewdae.com

SHYLLA WEBB

Shylla Webb, the founder of Inner Matter, believes people already have what they need within and is dedicated to showing leaders how to unlock their full potential to improve organizational well-being. She holds a master's degree in human behavior and guides leaders of various industries on how to lead with emotional intelligence, increase their performance, tap into the collective wisdom in a group, and create healthy team dynamics.

Her experience in transformational leadership, leading organizations, and her intuitive abilities enable Shylla to implement change in organizations in a fun and exciting way. She set out on a mission to coach using an experiential model, which makes learning new skills easier to imbed while performing our jobs. As a leader herself, she is ready to show you how to lead with inspiration and reach your full potential!

Connect with Shylla:

https://innermatter.com

JENNIFER HARSHMAN

Upbeat lover of language and learning Jennifer Harshman taught herself to read and write when she was three years old. She has consumed more than 20,000 books and developed an extremely broad knowledge base.

Jennifer attained degrees in psychology and education and has held a variety of leadership positions. She began helping authors professionally in 1992, developing more than 300 books and 30 million words so far, working around her children's special needs and her own. Some of her credits include *NYT* and *USA Today* bestsellers.

As a ghostwriter and author, she knows the struggles of writing. As a leader, she also knows how hard it can be to find the time to write. She created a "recipe" to simplify the process and make it fast and fun. Because of this, her coaching clients titled her The Book Baker®. Jennifer loves to help people like you achieve their goal of writing a book, so in addition to consulting would-be authors, she writes, teaches, and speaks about it. This is her third multi-author book (anthology), and she has more in the works.

Leaders should write, so contact Jennifer about your book today.

Connect with Jennifer:

Jennifer@HarshmanServices.com

https://www.HarshmanServices.com

https://www.YourBookBakery.com

https://www.Facebook.com/jennifer.harshman

https://www.TikTok.com/@jennifer_harshman

KENT SANDERS

Kent Sanders is the founder of Inkwell Ghostwriting, which helps leaders grow their business through books and other content. He is also the author and coauthor of numerous books, including *18 Words to Live By: A Father's Wisdom on What Matters Most* and co-author of *The Faith of Elvis: A Story Only a Brother Can Tell* with Billy Stanley, Elvis Presley's stepbrother.

Connect with Kent:

https://www.KentSanders.net

Helpful Books

The 4-Hour Work Week by Tim Ferriss—This book provides a framework for maximizing productivity and achieving a more balanced life.

Essentialism: The Disciplined Pursuit of Less by Greg McKeown—This book emphasizes the importance of focusing on what's most important and letting go of non-essential tasks.

The Power of Full Engagement by Jim Loehr and Tony Schwartz—This book teaches readers how to manage their energy levels to achieve a more balanced and fulfilling life.

The Healthy Workplace by Leigh Stringer—This book provides practical strategies for creating a workplace that supports the health and well-being of employees.

The Happiness Advantage by Shawn Achor—This book explores the connection between happiness and success, and provides practical tips for cultivating a positive and fulfilling life.

The 5 AM Club by Robin Sharma—This book focuses on building a morning routine to increase productivity and achieve a more balanced life.

Atomic Habits by James Clear—This book provides a framework for building small habits that can lead to big changes in work-life balance and overall well-being.

The One Thing by Gary Keller and Jay Papasan—This book teaches readers how to focus on one important task at a time to achieve greater productivity and balance in life.

The Art of Possibility by Rosamund Stone Zander and Benjamin Zander—This book provides a framework for shifting your mindset to focus on opportunities and possibilities, rather than limitations.

Mindfulness: An Eight-Week Plan for Finding Peace in a Frantic World by Mark Williams and Danny Penman—This book provides a step-by-step guide to practicing mindfulness, which can be a powerful tool for achieving greater balance and well-being in life.

Giftology by John Ruhlin—This book promises to give you higher profits and make marketing as natural as breathing and competition nearly nonexistent.